The Paralysis Instinct

Why You Can't Make Yourself Move Money You Know You Should Move

Jordan Ellis

First edition, 2026

Published by Jordan Ellis

Contents

Foreword 1

Introduction 3

Chapter 1 — The Account You Meant to Move 17

Chapter 2 — The Cash That's Just Sitting There 37

Chapter 3 — The Form You Keep Meaning to Sign 57

Chapter 4 — The Will You Haven't Written 75

Chapter 5 — The Rebalance You Keep Postponing 93

Chapter 6 — The Conversation You Keep Rescheduling 109

Chapter 7 — The Coverage You Know Is Wrong 127

Chapter 8 — The Raise That Never Reached Your Savings Rate 145

Chapter 9 — The Statement You Skim But Never Act On 163

Chapter 10 — The Five Minutes That Breaks the Freeze 181

Before You Go 199

Notes & Further Reading 205

About 215

Also in the Series 217

Foreword

I didn't notice the pattern in myself first. I noticed it in a man across a dinner table years ago, someone who ran a mid-sized business with real precision — he could quote his margins on any product line without checking a spreadsheet. Almost as an aside, he mentioned an old retirement account from a job he'd left nine years earlier, still sitting in funds he'd picked at twenty-six, funds he now admitted he wouldn't choose today. He knew exactly what to do about it. He'd known for years. He described the fifteen-minute phone call that would fix it with something close to affection — then he ordered another drink and the conversation moved on. Watching him, I understood the knowing wasn't the obstacle. He wasn't confused. He was stuck in a way that had nothing to do with information.

I went looking for my own version and found it embarrassingly fast. A form, sitting in a drawer for over a year, that would have taken four minutes to complete and would have closed a gap in exactly the kind of protection I'd tell anyone else to have in place. I knew what it said. I knew what to write on it.

I just hadn't, and the not-having-done-it had stopped registering as a task and started registering as a fact about the drawer, the way a stain on a rug eventually stops being something you mean to clean and starts being part of the rug.

This book exists because that gap — knowing exactly what to do, and not doing it — turns out to be far more common and far less understood than the dramatic financial failures that get written about. Nobody writes a chapter about the form in the drawer. There's no crash, no single bad decision to point to. Just years, quietly accumulating on top of a decision that was never actually made, only endlessly deferred.

I don't think the standard advice helps here, and I suspect you already know that, or you wouldn't have picked this up. "Just do it" has never once moved a stuck decision forward — if it worked, you'd have done it already. What actually helps is understanding why the freeze happens in a mind that already has every fact it needs. That's the only kind of help worth offering here, and it's what the rest of this book tries to do.

— Jordan Ellis

Introduction

You know exactly what you should do. That's the part that makes this different from almost every other money problem you'll ever read about. You're not confused about the old 401k sitting at a former employer — you know it needs to be rolled over, you've known for years, you could explain the mechanics of a rollover to a stranger at a dinner party without missing a step. You're not confused about the beneficiary form, the will, the rebalance, the coverage that's been wrong since a life event that happened three moves and one marriage ago. You could pass a quiz on every single one of these decisions right now, cold, with no notice. And you still haven't done any of them. Not because you're careless. Not because you don't understand the stakes. Because knowing what to do and doing it turn out to be two entirely different capacities, run by two entirely different systems, and one of them has been quietly winning for years without you ever agreeing to the arrangement.

This is the strangest kind of money trouble there is, because it doesn't look like trouble from the outside, or even from the inside, most days. There's no crisis. No red number flashing on a screen. No moment where a decision gets made badly and the damage announces itself. There's just a form, or an account, or a conversation, sitting exactly where it's been sitting, not getting worse in any way you can point to on any given Tuesday, and also never getting better. If a stranger asked you today what you should do about it, you'd answer instantly and correctly. If that same stranger asked why you haven't done it yet, you'd hear yourself reach for an answer that sounds reasonable and isn't quite true — busy, complicated, waiting for a better time — because the real answer, the one underneath the reasonable-sounding one, doesn't have language attached to it yet. That's what this book is for: giving that real answer a name, so you can finally do something about it other than wait.

It's worth being precise, right at the start, about what this book is not, because the two other closest subjects in this general territory are genuinely different problems, and confusing them will send you looking for the wrong fix. This is not a book about panic — about the acute, fast, event-triggered impulse to sell everything the instant a threat registers, hand moving before thought catches up. That's a real and separate reflex, fast and loud and over in minutes, and it deserves its own treatment, which exists elsewhere. This is also not a book about looking away — about the flinch before checking a balance, the unopened statement, the fear of what a number might confirm about your character. That's real too, and it's quiet in a completely different way: it's about not wanting to know. This book is about something that can only happen to someone who already knows. You've looked. You've read the statement. You understand the number, the form, the gap, completely. The freeze doesn't happen before the knowledge arrives. It happens after — sometimes years after — and that's precisely what makes it so disorienting to live inside. Panic is a reflex that outruns your thinking. Avoidance is a refusal to let the thinking start. This is neither. This is a decision that has all the information it needs, standing fully formed at the door, and simply never walking through it.

Consider two people, on two very different Tuesdays, whose situations look nothing alike and who are, underneath, running the identical pattern. The first is a woman in her late thirties, a data analyst, someone whose entire professional life is built around exactly the kind of precise, evidence-based decision-making this situation seems to call for. She has, sitting in a spreadsheet she built herself, a complete and accurate comparison of the old retirement account from a job she left four years ago against the new one at her current employer — fee structures laid out side by side, projected outcomes modeled to two decimal places, a clear and correct answer highlighted in the spreadsheet's own summary row. She built this spreadsheet fourteen months ago. She has opened it eleven times since, each time nodding at the same conclusion, each time closing the laptop without initiating the rollover the spreadsheet itself recommends. She is not missing information. She has more information than most professional advisors would bother assembling. What she's missing is something the spreadsheet was never built to provide, and she can't quite name what that something is, which is part of why the account is still sitting exactly where it was fourteen months ago.

The second is a man in his early sixties, a retired teacher, who has known for three years — since a conversation with his accountant that he still remembers almost word for word — that the beneficiary designation on his largest retirement account still names his first wife, from a marriage that ended eleven years ago, rather than his current wife of eight years, a mistake that would, if left uncorrected, hand a meaningful sum of money to someone who is no longer his spouse and quietly disinherit the person actually standing beside him. He has told this story to friends, at dinners, with a rueful little laugh, as though it were a charming personal quirk rather than a live legal error with real consequences — "I really need to get that fixed," he says, and everyone nods, and nobody, including him, treats the sentence as anything other than conversation. He is not confused about what the form requires. He filled out an identical form correctly, without hesitation, for a different account, six months ago. He simply has not touched this one, for three years, despite understanding the stakes better than almost anyone reading this book right now.

A third scene widens this further, because the freeze doesn't confine itself to individual accounts — sometimes it lives inside a household, shared and mutually reinforced by two people who each assume the other is closer to acting than they actually are.

A couple, several years into a marriage, sit through a financial planning session together and hear, plainly, from a professional they trust, that their current insurance coverage no longer matches their life — a policy sized for a couple with no children, now raising two, a gap significant enough that the advisor circles it twice on the printed summary and says, out loud, “this is the one thing I’d fix first.” They leave the meeting in full agreement. They talk about it in the car. And then, over the following eighteen months, each of them quietly assumes the other is handling it — she thinks he’s going to call the agent, since he handled the last policy; he thinks she’s going to call, since she’s the one who scheduled the planning session in the first place — and the account of who’s responsible drifts, unspoken, into a fog neither of them notices forming, until eighteen months become two years and the gap the advisor circled twice is still sitting there, uncircled by anyone, unfixed.

What connects all three of these people is the detail that makes this pattern so different from every other kind of financial mistake, and worth stating as plainly as possible before the book goes any further: none of them are ignorant. All three could pass a test on their own situation with a perfect score, today, without studying. The decision they haven't made isn't waiting on more research, more comparison, more understanding. It's waiting on something that has nothing to do with information at all — and that's precisely why more information, more spreadsheets, more reminders, more well-meaning advice from friends and professionals alike, keeps failing to move any of them. You cannot educate your way out of a freeze that was never caused by a lack of education in the first place.

Here is the book's central mechanism, stated as one clean sentence, because everything ahead is really just this sentence examined from ten different angles: your mind treats the choice to keep things exactly as they are as the one option that can never be blamed on you, and it will defend that option indefinitely, against any amount of evidence, because staying still feels — falsely, but powerfully — like the only decision you can't get wrong. This isn't laziness, and it isn't a character flaw, and it certainly isn't stupidity — every person in every scene in this book is, by any ordinary measure, sharp, capable, and fully informed. It's a specific, well-documented feature of how decisions actually get made under uncertainty, wired in long before spreadsheets or beneficiary forms existed, now running headlong into a modern financial life that requires dozens of active, deliberate, first-move decisions it was never built to comfortably supply.

It helps to understand, early, why this particular freeze deserves its own careful treatment rather than a chapter folded into a broader book about financial fear. General financial anxiety — the background hum of worry about not having enough, about the future being uncertain — is a real subject, and it behaves differently: chronic, diffuse, present even when there's nothing specific to point to. What this book covers is narrower and, in a strange way, more precise: a specific decision, fully understood, sitting untouched, indefinitely, without the reader ever having consciously decided *not* to act. Nobody wakes up one morning and declares, out loud or even privately, "I've decided not to roll over that account" or "I've decided not to fix that beneficiary form." The decision to not-decide is never actually made. It just accumulates, one deferred Tuesday at a time, until years have passed and the account is exactly where it started, and the only thing that's changed is how long the excuse has had to calcify into something that no longer even feels like an excuse — it feels like a fact about you, the way "I'm just someone who hasn't gotten to that yet" starts to feel like a permanent trait rather than a temporary state.

Each chapter ahead takes one specific, recognizable shape this freeze wears — the old account left behind, the cash sitting uninvested because there are too many good options to choose between, the form that never gets signed, the will that never gets written, the rebalance that never happens, the conversation that keeps getting rescheduled, the coverage everyone agrees is wrong, the raise that never reaches the savings rate, the statement that gets read but never acted on — and does the same five things with it. Opens with a close, specific scene, so you recognize the shape rather than a stranger's cautionary tale. Names the real, researched mechanism underneath it, credited honestly to the actual psychologists and economists who studied it, never invented for effect. Counts what the pattern actually costs, in dollars and in something quieter. Hands you concrete, specific overrides — not general encouragement to "just do it," which has never once worked on anyone, but small, structural changes to how the decision gets set up, so that acting becomes the path of least resistance instead of staying frozen. And closes with a single line worth carrying forward, distilled from everything the chapter just walked through.

It's worth being honest about something before the first chapter begins, because it will shape how you read everything that follows: this book will not make you a person who suddenly enjoys making financial decisions, and it will not hand you some new, endless supply of motivation you didn't have before. Motivation was never the missing ingredient — every person in this book already wanted to act, in the ordinary sense of wanting, and wanting alone clearly wasn't enough, or the accounts wouldn't still be sitting there. What this book offers instead is a working understanding of exactly where the freeze happens in the decision chain, chapter by chapter, mechanism by mechanism, so you can build something concrete at that exact point rather than continuing to hope that one day you'll simply feel ready. Readiness, it turns out, is rarely the thing that produces action. Structure is. This book is an attempt to hand you that structure, piece by piece, using real research rather than motivational language, because motivational language is precisely the thing that hasn't worked on you yet, or you wouldn't be reading this.

One more thing before the chapters begin, because it matters for how you'll use what follows. You are very likely to recognize yourself in more than one chapter — possibly most of them. The freeze doesn't confine itself to a single account or a single kind of decision once it's found a foothold; a person who's left one account unrolled for years is statistically likely to also be sitting on an unfixed beneficiary form, an unwritten will, a rebalance nobody's gotten to. That's not a coincidence, and it's not a personal failing stacking on top of itself. It's the same underlying mechanism, wearing different financial clothes in different corners of the same life. Read for the chapters that land hardest. Don't be surprised if that's more than one.

A word about the research grounding this book relies on, because it matters for how much weight you give to what follows. Every mechanism named in these pages comes from a real, published, peer-reviewed body of work, credited to the specific researchers who actually did it — not a secondhand summary, not an invented statistic dressed up to sound authoritative. Where a finding is well-established and widely replicated, this book says so. Where a finding is newer or narrower in scope, this book says that too. You will not find a single claim in these chapters along the lines of "studies show" with no name attached, because a claim like that is worth exactly nothing, and readers of this kind of book have been burned by that phrase too many times to be handed another version of it here. The scenes, by contrast — the people, the accounts, the specific Tuesdays — are composites, built from recognizable, widespread patterns rather than any single person's exact history, because the point of a scene like this isn't documentary accuracy about one individual. It's recognition. You should be able to see a piece of your own life in at least one of them, not because your life was studied, but because the pattern is common enough that a careful, honest composite can capture it faithfully.

It's also worth saying plainly what this book expects of you as a reader, because it's different from what most books in this general category ask. Most personal-finance books ask for your attention and your willingness to change a behavior. This one asks for something slightly different and, in a specific way, slightly harder: your willingness to notice, honestly, which of the ten patterns ahead is already running in your own life right now, today, without waiting for the "right" chapter to arrive before admitting it. Several of the scenes in this book will likely feel uncomfortably close. That discomfort isn't a flaw in the writing. It's the whole mechanism working exactly as intended — recognition is the first and most necessary step in a process that has, until now, been running entirely below your own awareness.

Let's start where this pattern always starts — not with the decision itself, but with the much older, much simpler preference your mind holds for whatever is already true, simply because it's already true.

Chapter 1 — The Account You Meant to Move

Why Full Information Doesn't Produce Action

She has the number pulled up twice a year, almost like clockwork, usually sometime around the New Year and again sometime in early summer — a small, private ritual she's never mentioned to anyone, not because it's secret exactly, but because saying it out loud would mean admitting how long it's been going on. The account is from a job she left four years ago, a job she was, by any measure, glad to leave, at a company whose name barely registers anymore when she sees it on old tax documents. The account itself has done fine — she checked, actually checked, not just glanced — sitting in a target-date fund that's grown steadily, unremarkably, exactly the way it was supposed to. That's not the problem. The problem, which she can recite without notes, is that the fee structure at her old employer's plan runs meaningfully higher than what she'd pay if she rolled the balance into her current employer's plan, or into an account of her own choosing — a gap that, run out over the number of years she has left until retirement, adds up to a genuinely large sum, large enough that she built an actual spreadsheet fourteen months ago specifically to calculate it, because the number felt too consequential to eyeball.

She opens that spreadsheet again this January, the twelfth time now by her own rough count, and the answer hasn't changed, because nothing about her situation has changed enough to change it. Roll it over. It's still the obviously correct move, stated in her own handwriting at the bottom of her own analysis. She reads the recommendation, nods — actually nods, alone in her kitchen, a small physical gesture of agreement with a document she wrote herself — and then closes the laptop and makes coffee and goes about the rest of her Tuesday exactly as if the account weren't sitting there at all. She isn't confused. She isn't even particularly anxious about it, most days — it's not a live source of dread the way an unopened bill might be. It's just sitting there, technically pending, permanently pending, in a category of task that has stopped feeling like a task and started feeling like a fact about her life, the way "I have an account at my old job" has quietly become as unremarkable a sentence as "I have a car" or "I have a dentist."

A second scene shows the same freeze wearing a slightly different costume, useful because it removes the excuse of complexity entirely. A man in his late twenties, recently promoted, receives a straightforward, unambiguous email from his company's HR department: his new compensation tier makes him eligible for a better employer match on his retirement contributions, but only if he actively logs into the benefits portal and re-elects his contribution percentage — a task the email estimates, accurately, at under three minutes. He reads the email standing in a hallway between meetings, understands it completely, forwards it to himself with a note that says "do this tonight," and then does not do it that night, or the following week, or the following month. Six months later, doing an unrelated year-end review of his benefits, he discovers the re-election never happened, and calculates, with a flat, unsurprised kind of dread, exactly how much in matched contributions he's left on the table during those six months — a real, calculable number, sitting in an account it will now never occupy, lost not to a bad decision but to the complete absence of a three-minute one.

A third scene belongs here as well, because the pattern doesn't only affect individual accounts — it shows up just as reliably in decisions two people share, where each assumes the pending task belongs, at least partly, to someone else. A small business, co-owned by two partners for eleven years, has been operating under a buy-sell agreement drafted when the business was worth a fraction of its current value — a document both partners know, with total clarity, no longer reflects reality, and both partners have separately raised, at separate points, over separate years, the need to have it redrafted by an attorney. Neither has ever actually scheduled the appointment. Each assumes, quietly, that raising the topic again constitutes meaningful progress, that the conversation itself is a kind of action, when in fact eleven years of agreeing the document is wrong has produced exactly zero changes to the document itself. The agreement sits, technically valid, functionally obsolete, protecting neither partner in the way either of them believes it does, not because either one doubts what needs to happen, but because "we should really deal with that" has been mistaken, by both of them, for actually dealing with it.

A fourth scene shows the identical status quo bias operating on a much smaller, almost mundane decision, useful because it demonstrates the mechanism doesn't require significant stakes to take hold. A young professional has kept a checking account at a bank he actively dislikes for three years, well past the point where he found a credit union offering meaningfully better terms and, by his own estimate, better service — a switch he describes, when it comes up, as something he's "been meaning to do." The actual barrier isn't complexity; moving a direct deposit and a handful of automatic payments is a well-understood, one-afternoon task he could complete without much difficulty. It's that the current account, however disliked, has become the invisible plumbing everything else in his financial life runs through, and touching plumbing that currently works, however imperfectly, triggers the same reluctance this chapter has described in far higher-stakes settings — proof that the status quo bias scales down as readily as it scales up, defending a mediocre checking account with the same basic mechanism it uses to defend a six-figure retirement account.

What's actually happening

The economists William Samuelson and Richard Zeckhauser gave this pattern its formal name in a landmark 1988 paper: the status quo bias. Their research, built on a series of controlled decision experiments, found something that ran against how economists had traditionally assumed people made choices — that when people face a decision with multiple reasonable options, they show a strong, measurable, systematic preference for whichever option represents "staying as things currently are," even when the alternatives are objectively presented as equal or better, and even when switching would cost the person nothing more than a small amount of effort. Notably, Samuelson and Zeckhauser found this bias grew stronger, not weaker, as the number of alternatives increased and as the decision grew more complex — meaning the exact situations most in need of a deliberate, active choice are the ones the status quo bias defends most fiercely. The old 401k, sitting quietly among several plausible destinations for the money, isn't a simple case where the bias would be expected to be weak. It's precisely the kind of multi-option, moderately complex decision where their research found the pull toward "leave it exactly where it is" strongest.

It's worth understanding why this bias exists at all, because it isn't simply carelessness dressed up in academic language — there's a real, defensible logic underneath it, even if that logic misfires badly in a modern financial context. Samuelson and Zeckhauser's own explanation drew partly on a companion finding from behavioral economics: that people evaluate potential losses and potential gains asymmetrically, weighing a possible loss more heavily than an equivalent possible gain. Applied to a decision like a rollover, this asymmetry does something specific and important: it makes the *possible* downsides of switching — a paperwork error, an unexpected tax consequence, a fund that underperforms the one you left — loom disproportionately large in the mind, while the *certain*, already-being-paid cost of staying put barely registers at all, precisely because it isn't new, isn't a fresh loss, isn't something that would require blaming yourself for a specific action taken on a specific day. Staying still doesn't feel like choosing the worse of two options. It feels like not choosing at all, and not choosing, to a mind wired to weigh losses harder than gains, feels like the only genuinely safe position on the board.

There's a further layer to Samuelson and Zeckhauser's findings worth naming directly, because it explains why the account sitting at an old employer feels different, psychologically, from a fresh decision presented for the first time. Their research distinguished between decisions framed as "choose one of these options" and decisions where one option was pre-installed as the existing arrangement — and found the preference for the pre-installed option held even when participants had, moments earlier, expressed a genuine preference for a different one in the abstract. In other words, simply being the *current* arrangement gives an option a psychological weight that has nothing to do with its actual merits. The old 401k isn't winning because it's the better choice. It's winning because it doesn't have to be chosen at all — it just has to not be actively un-chosen, and un-choosing something turns out to require a specific, deliberate kind of effort that choosing a fresh option, oddly, doesn't.

This connects directly to a second, closely related body of research that explains why the man in the hallway — someone facing a task with no complexity at all, just a simple three-minute form — still failed to act. The economists Brigitte Madrian and Dennis Shea, studying retirement plan enrollment at a large company in a 2001 study published in the *Quarterly Journal of Economics*, found something striking about default settings specifically: when a company switched from requiring employees to actively opt in to a retirement plan, to instead automatically enrolling employees unless they actively opted out, participation rates jumped dramatically — not because employees' underlying preferences about saving had changed, but because the default itself, whatever it happened to be, exerted an enormous, largely invisible gravitational pull on the eventual outcome. Madrian and Shea's finding matters enormously here because it shows the status quo bias isn't limited to decisions about *existing* accounts. It governs blank, unfilled defaults too — the man's benefits portal defaulted to his old contribution percentage until he actively changed it, and that default, sitting quietly unchosen, won the same way the old 401k wins: not through anyone's active preference, but through the simple, powerful fact of requiring no action to remain in force.

There's a further wrinkle in Madrian and Shea's broader body of research worth naming, because it speaks directly to the buy-sell agreement scene: the pull of a default gets stronger, not weaker, the more the decision touches an area a person finds effortful or emotionally loaded to think about carefully — and legal and financial documents reliably rank among the most effortful, least emotionally comfortable categories most people ever have to engage with voluntarily. Two capable business partners, each individually decisive in running daily operations, can still defer an eleven-year-old legal document specifically because the *category* of task — legal, financial, requiring an outside professional, requiring a conversation neither wants to initiate first — carries enough friction on its own that the default of "leave it as it is" wins by default, quite literally, without either partner ever consciously choosing it.

It's worth being precise about what all three scenes share, because the shared structure is the actual subject of this chapter. In every case, the person facing the frozen decision had complete, accurate information about what the correct action was. None of them were confused. None of them needed a spreadsheet built, a call scheduled, an expert consulted to determine the right answer — the woman's spreadsheet already existed, the man's email already spelled out the exact steps, the partners had already agreed, more than once, on what the document needed to say. What none of them had was a mechanism that made the correct action the *effortless* one, and in the absence of that mechanism, the status quo — requiring nothing, risking nothing new, blaming no one — kept winning by simply outlasting everyone's good intentions.

There's a related finding worth adding here, because it explains why the pull toward the old account feels different from ordinary indifference — why it doesn't feel neutral, the way leaving a truly unimportant decision unmade might feel. The endowment effect, first documented in a series of experiments by Daniel Kahneman, Jack Knetsch, and Richard Thaler in a 1990 paper, found that people consistently assign higher value to something simply because they already own it, compared to the value they'd assign to the identical item if they didn't yet own it and were considering acquiring it fresh. Applied to a retirement account, this means the old 401k isn't experienced as a neutral pile of money waiting to be optimally placed. It's experienced, subtly, as *hers* — already claimed, already familiar, already carrying a kind of psychological ownership that a freshly opened account at a new provider hasn't yet earned, even though the actual underlying investments could be structured identically in either location. The endowment effect and the status quo bias reinforce each other here, each one making the other harder to see clearly: staying put isn't just effortless, it's defended by a felt sense that the current account has already become something worth more than its dollar value alone would suggest, simply by virtue of having been held.

It's worth being specific about how this compounds over time rather than staying constant. Samuelson and Zeckhauser's original research found that the strength of the status quo bias in a given decision correlates with how long the current arrangement has already been in place — a finding with an uncomfortable implication for anyone reading this chapter and recognizing their own frozen account. The bias isn't static. Every additional year an account sits unrolled doesn't just represent another year of foregone savings; it represents another year of the status quo bias itself growing stronger, making the eventual correction, whenever it finally happens, feel like it requires overcoming an even larger psychological hurdle than it would have the year before. This is precisely backward from how most people intuitively think about a task like this — the natural assumption is that delay is at worst neutral, simply postponing an unchanged decision. The research suggests delay is actively corrosive, hardening the very default it's failing to correct.

What it costs you

The financial cost is the easiest to quantify, and it's worth doing the math plainly, because vague awareness of "some cost" rarely moves anyone the way a concrete figure does. A meaningful gap in fees, run out across years of continued growth, compounds the same way any investment cost compounds — quietly, invisibly, in a direction you never see because there's no single moment where the loss registers as a loss. It doesn't look like money leaving an account. It looks like an account growing a little more slowly than it otherwise would have, year after year, in a way that's essentially impossible to notice without doing the exact side-by-side comparison the woman in this chapter's opening scene has already done, twelve times, and acted on zero.

There's a second cost, less visible but arguably more corrosive over time: every deferred decision that gets revisited and re-deferred strengthens the neural and behavioral pathway that produces the deferral in the first place. This isn't a metaphor. Behavior that gets repeated, particularly behavior that successfully avoids an uncomfortable action and gets rewarded with the immediate relief of not having to do the effortful thing, tends to become more automatic with repetition, not less — a basic principle of how habits form, whether the habit in question is a good one or a costly one. The woman's twelfth look at her spreadsheet isn't neutral. It's practice at looking-and-not-acting, and each rehearsal makes the thirteenth easier to skip past unbothered, which is precisely backward from what she'd want if she thought about it directly.

A third cost compounds across an entire financial life rather than staying contained to any single account: once the status quo bias wins on one decision, it tends to generalize, quietly expanding its territory into every other pending decision nearby. The account left unrolled makes the beneficiary form easier to leave unfixed, which makes the will easier to leave unwritten, not because any of these decisions are actually connected to each other in substance, but because a mind that has successfully defended "leave it as it is" once starts treating that defense as the reasonable default response to financial decisions generally, applying it more broadly than any single instance would justify on its own.

A fourth cost only becomes visible at a household or family level rather than an individual one: a scattered collection of old, unrolled accounts — one from this job, one from that one, each left in place by the identical mechanism this chapter has described — creates a specific administrative burden that eventually lands on someone other than the person who left them there. A spouse, an adult child, or an executor eventually managing an estate or a divorce or simply trying to get a clear picture of a household's total financial position inherits the accumulated cost of every account nobody ever consolidated, often without any record of why each one was left exactly where it was. The status quo bias doesn't just cost the person experiencing it. Left unaddressed long enough, it quietly transfers a real, concrete cost onto whoever eventually has to untangle it, at a moment — a death, a divorce, a health crisis — when untangling anything is hardest.

The overrides

Convert the decision from "should I switch" into "actively re-choose to stay, in writing, with a reason." This inverts the default entirely. Instead of the status quo requiring zero effort and the switch requiring all of it, force the status quo to require its own act of justification. Set a specific date, put it on a calendar, and commit that on that date you will either complete the rollover or write down, in one full sentence, the specific reason staying makes more sense than moving. Most people find this second option nearly impossible to write honestly — there usually isn't a real reason, only the absence of one — and the difficulty of writing that sentence is itself the diagnostic. If you can't justify staying in writing, you've just demonstrated to yourself, cheaply and quickly, that the status quo has been winning on inertia alone.

The Move: shrink the task to its smallest possible physical unit, and do only that unit today. Not "roll over the account" — that's the version that's been sitting undone for fourteen months precisely because it reads as one large, effortful task. Instead: today, find the phone number or the login. That's the entire task. Not the call, not the form, not the transfer — just locating the single piece of information required to start. This works because the status quo bias defends against effortful, ambiguous tasks far more successfully than it defends against a task so small it barely qualifies as a task at all. Once the phone number is found, the next smallest unit — making the call — becomes measurably easier to face, because a piece of the resistance has already been spent on something trivial.

Borrow Madrian and Shea's finding and build your own default in the other direction. If your employer, bank, or plan provider offers any kind of automatic or scheduled action — an automatic transfer, a standing appointment, a recurring reminder that requires you to actively cancel it rather than actively initiate it — use it deliberately, specifically because defaults are powerful regardless of which direction they point. You cannot delete the status quo bias from your own wiring. You can, however, choose which status quo it's defending, by building the correct action into a system that runs unless you actively stop it, rather than one that stays dormant unless you actively start it.

Assign the pending decision an actual owner, out loud, if it's shared. If a decision belongs to more than one person — a couple, business partners, family members handling a shared account — the diffusion of responsibility itself becomes part of what feeds the freeze; each person's inaction feels justified by the other's, and neither one ever experiences the decision as fully theirs to move. Name a single owner explicitly, in a specific conversation, with a specific deadline attached to that one person's name. A decision with one clear owner and one clear date behaves completely differently than the identical decision left as "something we should really get to."

Notice, and interrupt, the ritual of revisiting without resolving. If you find yourself returning to the same spreadsheet, the same account summary, the same mental review of a decision you've already reached, without that review ever ending in action, treat the review itself as a warning sign rather than as progress. Reviewing isn't neutral. It's rehearsal — and rehearsing the decision without executing it trains the exact pattern this chapter has been describing. The next time you catch yourself opening that familiar tab, ask directly: am I gathering new information, or am I just practicing not acting on the information I already have?

Run a five-year forward test before defending the status quo. If you catch yourself justifying inaction, ask directly: if I opened this exact account fresh today, with no history attached to it, would I choose to build it exactly the way it currently sits? If the honest answer is no, the only thing keeping the current arrangement in place is the endowment effect described above, not any actual merit of its own — and that's worth naming plainly before letting another year pass on the strength of a preference that only exists because you already own it.

The Rule to Remember: Staying still isn't the safe choice — it's just the choice that doesn't feel like one, and it costs exactly as much as any other decision you make by not

making it.

Chapter 2 — The Cash That's Just Sitting There

Why More Options Make You Choose Nothing

The number in the checking account has been climbing for a while now, slowly, unremarkably, the way a number climbs when a person is doing reasonably well and simply isn't spending it as fast as it arrives. She noticed it first almost by accident, glancing at a total she wasn't specifically looking for, and felt a small, genuine jolt of surprise at how large it had gotten — large enough that she opened a calculator app right there in the grocery store parking lot and did some quick, rough math on what that same sum could be earning somewhere else, invested rather than simply sitting, doing nothing but slowly losing ground to inflation the way idle cash always does. She knows this. She's known it for months. She isn't confused about the fact that money sitting in a low-interest checking account is, in the plainest financial sense, quietly losing value every single day it sits there uninvested.

What stops her isn't the concept. It's the specifics. The moment she opens her brokerage app to actually move the money somewhere, she's confronted with a list of choices that seems to multiply the longer she looks at it — a handful of broad index options, several target-date funds pegged to different retirement years, a robo-advisor tool offering to build a custom allocation based on a short quiz, articles linked from the app itself comparing approaches with headlines that all sound equally confident and equally at odds with each other. She reads three of these articles standing in her kitchen, feels reasonably informed after the first one, less informed after the second one contradicts a detail from the first, and genuinely uncertain after the third one introduces a consideration neither of the others mentioned. She closes the app. The money stays exactly where it was, not because she's decided checking is the right place for it, but because every specific alternative she looked at came with just enough of its own complexity that none of them felt like the obviously correct next step, and "obviously correct" was the bar she'd unconsciously set for herself before she'd start moving anything.

A second scene, involving a completely different sum and a completely different life stage, shows the identical mechanism at a smaller scale. A young man in his mid-twenties receives an unexpected bonus at the end of a strong year — not life-changing money, but a real, meaningful sum, more than he's ever had to actively decide what to do with in one lump. He knows, in the broad strokes, that he should probably split it between paying down a modest amount of remaining student debt and starting to invest, and he knows this the way most financially literate young adults know it: correctly, but without a specific plan for exactly how to split it, exactly which account to use for the investing half, exactly whether to prioritize the debt first or invest first given the specific interest rate on the loan versus the historical return of the market. He opens four different tabs comparing these exact questions, reads conflicting takes from what appear to be equally credible sources, and eventually — not from any conclusion, but from simple fatigue — closes all four tabs and leaves the bonus sitting in the checking account it landed in, where it remains, doing nothing, eleven months later.

A third scene rounds this out, because the freeze here doesn't require an unusual sum at all — it can happen with an entirely ordinary amount, simply because the number of paths forward feels disproportionate to the size of the decision. A retired couple, having just consolidated several small old accounts into one larger one as part of a routine cleanup, sit down together with the resulting balance and a genuine, shared intention to decide, once and for all, how it should be allocated going forward. They've done this kind of thing before, successfully, with smaller amounts. But this particular sitting-down happens to coincide with a period where they've each, independently, read a different article recommending a different approach — one favoring a more conservative, income-focused allocation given their age, the other favoring a more growth-oriented approach given how many years they realistically have left to draw on the money. Neither article is wrong, exactly. They simply point in different directions, and rather than pick one and adjust later if needed, the couple tables the conversation "until we've both had more time to think about it," a sentence that, eight months later, still accurately describes where things stand, and where the money, unchanged, continues to sit.

A fourth scene belongs here too, because it shows the freeze surviving even genuine professional help, which is worth naming since it's the recommendation most people reach for first when they notice they're stuck. A freelance graphic designer, after a particularly strong year, finally hires a fee-only financial planner specifically to get past exactly this kind of paralysis — a real, meaningful cash cushion that's been sitting uninvested for over a year, growing steadily through her own income but earning almost nothing from where it sits. The planner does excellent, genuinely useful work: builds a clear, well-reasoned allocation recommendation, walks her through it carefully, answers every question she raises. She leaves the meeting with a specific, actionable plan, fully understood, fully agreed to. Four months later, the plan still hasn't been executed, not because she's changed her mind about it, but because implementing it requires her own active follow-through — opening a specific account, initiating a specific transfer — and that follow-through has quietly joined the same queue of good intentions everything else in this chapter has described. Hiring the right professional solved the choice-overload problem entirely. It didn't solve the separate, distinct problem of converting a resolved choice into an executed one, which turns out to be exactly the gap this book's final chapter is built to close.

What's actually happening

The psychologists Sheena Iyengar and Mark Lepper ran an experiment in 2000 that has become one of the most widely cited findings in the study of choice — an experiment involving, of all things, jam. Set up as a tasting table at an upscale grocery store, the researchers alternated between offering shoppers a selection of six jam varieties to sample and, on different days, a selection of twenty-four. The larger display drew significantly more people over to look — a bigger, more impressive array is, unsurprisingly, more attention-grabbing. But when it came to actually buying a jar afterward, the pattern reversed sharply: shoppers who'd sampled from the smaller selection of six were roughly ten times more likely to make a purchase than shoppers who'd sampled from the larger selection of twenty-four. More options drew more interest and produced dramatically less action. Iyengar and Lepper's broader research program, extending well beyond jam into more consequential domains including retirement plan enrollment, found the same basic pattern repeating: as the number of available options grows past a certain point, the cognitive and emotional effort required to compare them all thoroughly enough to feel confident in a choice grows faster than most people's willingness to actually do that comparing, and the easiest way to resolve that mismatch, for a great many people, isn't to pick imperfectly — it's to not pick at all.

It's worth understanding precisely why this happens, because the mechanism isn't simply "too many choices is overwhelming," stated vaguely. Iyengar and Lepper's work, and the substantial body of choice-overload research that followed it, points to a more specific culprit: the fear of a wrong choice grows in direct proportion to the number of alternatives available, because more alternatives means more specific, nameable ways the choice you eventually make could turn out to have been the wrong one. With six jam options, choosing the fifth-best one still feels like a reasonably good outcome — you can imagine, roughly, what you might have missed, and it doesn't feel catastrophic. With twenty-four options, choosing what turns out to be the eighteenth-best one feels different, sharper, more like a specific, countable failure, even though the actual difference in jam quality between the fifth-best and the eighteenth-best of twenty-four options is, in most real cases, genuinely negligible. The proliferation of options doesn't just make comparison harder. It manufactures a much larger, more vivid set of specific regrets to anticipate, and anticipating regret, it turns out, is enough on its own to freeze a decision that would otherwise be simple.

This connects directly to a related and highly relevant finding from psychologist Barry Schwartz, working with Iyengar and several co-authors in a 2002 paper distinguishing between two decision-making styles: maximizing and satisficing — a distinction that traces back originally to the economist Herbert Simon's foundational 1956 work on bounded rationality, which argued that fully optimal decision-making is often practically impossible given real limits on time, information, and cognitive capacity, and that a rational actor under those real-world constraints should aim not for the theoretically perfect choice but for one that's good enough to meet a clear standard. Schwartz's research found that people who approach decisions as maximizers — searching exhaustively for the single best option among all available alternatives — report significantly more regret, more anxiety during the decision process, and, counterintuitively, less satisfaction with whatever choice they eventually do make, compared to people who approach the same decisions as satisficers, willing to select the first option that clearly meets a reasonable bar and move on. The woman standing in her kitchen reading a third article isn't failing to find the best fund. She's succeeded, unwittingly, at becoming a maximizer in a domain where maximizing behavior reliably produces paralysis rather than optimal outcomes — because the actual difference in long-run results between several reasonable, well-diversified options is, for the vast majority of people, far smaller than the cost of the months or years spent uninvested while searching for certainty that the research itself suggests doesn't meaningfully exist to be found.

There's a further layer worth adding, because it explains why cash specifically — as opposed to, say, a decision about which car to buy — proves so uniquely resistant to resolution. Iyengar's later research on retirement savings decisions, examining actual employee participation data across a large number of company plans, found that participation rates in voluntary retirement plans dropped measurably as the number of available fund options in the plan increased, following the same basic shape as the jam finding, but with meaningfully higher real-world stakes attached to each individual's non-decision. Tellingly, this later research found the effect strongest not among people with the least financial sophistication, but among people with moderate financial knowledge — enough to recognize that the choice actually mattered and deserved real consideration, not enough to feel fully confident making that consideration quickly. This is precisely the profile of the people in this chapter's scenes: informed enough to know cash sitting idle is a real cost, informed enough to recognize genuine tradeoffs between reasonable alternatives, and therefore squarely inside the zone where choice overload does its most effective freezing.

It's worth naming, too, why the couple's situation — two people, two competing articles, a shared decision — produces a freeze that's arguably harder to break than either individual scene. When a choice-overload freeze happens to one person, at least one path exists in principle: pick anything reasonable and move on. When it happens to two people who've each independently anchored to a different reasonable-sounding recommendation, resolving the freeze now requires not just picking an option, but one person accepting that the other's preferred article was, in some sense, the less compelling one — a social cost layered directly on top of the underlying choice-overload cost, which helps explain why "we'll decide together later" so often becomes the couple's own version of the status quo bias, defended by neither person wanting to be the one who pushed for their own preference over their partner's.

There's a further finding from Iyengar's broader body of work worth adding, because it clarifies exactly which kind of complexity does the most damage. Her research distinguished between the sheer *number* of options and the *comparability* of those options — finding that a large number of easily comparable alternatives produces meaningfully less freeze than a smaller number of alternatives that are each structured differently enough that comparing them requires real, sustained cognitive effort. This matters directly for the woman standing in her kitchen: her actual menu of choices wasn't simply long, it was heterogeneous — index funds, target-date funds, a quiz-based robo-advisor tool, each one requiring a different mental framework just to evaluate on its own terms before any cross-comparison could even begin. It wasn't twenty-four jars of jam sitting side by side on one table, directly comparable at a glance. It was several entirely different kinds of decisions, dressed up to look like one decision, and Iyengar's research suggests this specific structure — options that require translation before they can even be compared — produces freeze at a lower absolute number of choices than a simpler, more homogeneous set would.

What it costs you

The most direct cost is the one that's easiest to calculate and easiest to underestimate: money sitting in a low-yield account, uninvested, for months or years, loses real purchasing power to inflation and forgoes whatever growth it would otherwise have captured, and this cost compounds the longer the freeze lasts — a decision deferred for eleven months costs meaningfully more than the identical decision deferred for one, not because the underlying choice got harder, but because more time simply passed with the money doing nothing.

There's a subtler cost specific to this chapter's mechanism worth naming directly: every time a maximizing search ends in no decision rather than an imperfect one, it reinforces the belief that more research is always the responsible move — a belief that sounds virtuous and is, in this specific context, actively counterproductive. The genuinely responsible move, once a decision has cleared a reasonable bar of due diligence, is to act on it and revisit later if warranted. Continuing to search past that point isn't diligence. It's a costume diligence wears while the actual function it's serving is delay.

A third cost shows up specifically in shared decisions like the retired couple's: an unresolved choice-overload freeze inside a partnership doesn't stay static — it quietly starts generating a low, ambient tension that has nothing to do with either person's actual financial judgment and everything to do with the accumulated weight of an open question neither person wants to be the one to close. Left long enough, “we haven’t decided yet” stops sounding like a temporary state and starts sounding, to both people, like evidence that the couple simply isn’t good at making financial decisions together — a conclusion neither the six-option jam table nor the twenty-four-option one would ever actually support, but one that feels increasingly hard to argue with the longer the specific freeze goes unaddressed.

A fourth cost compounds specifically because cash is unusually easy to leave in place compared to almost anything else in this book. A frozen decision about a will or a form eventually forces itself back into view — an attorney follows up, a deadline approaches, a life event intrudes. Idle cash rarely announces itself this way. A checking account balance that’s grown comfortably large doesn’t send a reminder, doesn’t trigger a deadline, doesn’t create any visible friction at all; it simply sits, quietly available for ordinary spending, which means the choice-overload freeze covered in this chapter can persist far longer, with far less external pressure to resolve it, than almost any other pattern in this book. The absence of a forcing function isn't a minor detail. It's the specific reason cash-sitting-idle can run for years rather than months, undisturbed by anything except an occasional grocery-store-parking-lot moment of noticing.

One thing worth naming before the overrides: none of what follows asks you to research less thoroughly, or to care less about getting a good outcome. It asks you to separate the research phase from the decision phase, deliberately, because Iyengar and Schwartz's combined research suggests the two, left to blend together indefinitely, don't actually improve each other — they just extend each other, past the point where either one is still adding real value.

The overrides

Pre-commit to a decision rule before you look at the options, not after. Before opening any app, article, or list of alternatives, decide in advance what "good enough" looks like — a specific, simple standard, such as "a broadly diversified, low-cost option matching my approximate time horizon" — and commit that the first option meeting that standard is the one you'll choose, full stop. This inverts the maximizing search before it can start, because the standard exists before the options do, rather than being built reactively out of whichever comparison you happen to read first.

The Move: artificially shrink the option set to three before you evaluate anything. Whatever the actual menu of choices looks like — six funds, twenty-four, an entire brokerage's worth of products — pick three, using any reasonable, quick filter (lowest fees, broadest diversification, whatever criterion you trust most), and refuse to look at anything outside those three. This directly counters Iyengar and Lepper's finding: a smaller, deliberately bounded set produces dramatically higher completion rates than an open-ended one, even when the open-ended set technically contains a "better" option somewhere inside it. A good decision made from three is worth more than a perfect decision endlessly pending from twenty-four.

Set a maximizing budget, in minutes, and stop when it runs out. Give yourself an explicit, generous-but-finite amount of research time — ninety minutes, say, across a single week — and treat the end of that budget as the decision deadline, not a suggestion. When the budget runs out, you act on whatever your best current understanding supports, even if it doesn't feel like the fully optimal answer. Schwartz's research on maximizing suggests the difference in actual outcome between the option chosen after ninety minutes and the option that might theoretically have been found after ninety hours is, for the overwhelming majority of real financial decisions, far smaller than the cost of the extra eighty-eight and a half hours spent uninvested.

Split the decision to lower the stakes of any single choice. If part of what's freezing you is the fear of picking the single wrong destination for the entire sum, remove that specific fear by deliberately splitting the money across two or three of your shortlisted options rather than requiring yourself to pick exactly one. This isn't optimal portfolio construction advice — it's a psychological tool, and a legitimate one: a decision that no longer requires certainty about a single best answer is measurably easier to actually make than one that does.

If the freeze is shared, split the decision-making role explicitly rather than requiring full agreement on everything. A couple or shared-account holder doesn't need identical conviction on every choice to move forward together. Assign one person to narrow the field using an agreed-upon rule, and the other to make the final pick from that narrowed field — a structure that turns an open-ended joint search, which tends to freeze precisely because it has no natural endpoint, into a bounded process with a clear final step and a clear person responsible for taking it.

Name the specific regret you're actually avoiding, out loud, before you keep searching. Choice-overload freeze is often really an unexamined fear of one specific regret — picking the option that underperforms, missing a better fee structure, choosing wrong in front of a partner. Naming that specific fear directly, rather than letting it stay a vague background unease, frequently reveals it to be smaller and more survivable than the indefinite delay it's been producing, since the actual dollar difference between reasonable options is nearly always modest compared to the cost of staying in cash.

The Rule to Remember: More good options were never the same thing as more clarity — past a certain point, they're the same thing as no decision at all.

Chapter 3 — The Form You Keep Meaning to Sign

Why Doing Nothing Feels Safer Than Doing Something Wrong

The form has lived in the same manila folder for two years now, tucked behind a stack of other documents that get pulled out and refiled regularly, so that the folder itself isn't neglected — it's opened often, handled often, just never quite all the way to the bottom, where this particular form sits. He knows what it is. He knows what it's for. It's a change-of-beneficiary form for a life insurance policy he took out shortly after his first child was born, a policy that still names, as its sole beneficiary, an estate structure that made sense at the time and stopped making sense the moment his second child arrived three years later, since when nothing about the form has changed, despite two separate conversations with an attorney friend, both of whom told him plainly that the current setup would create real complications — delays, taxes, a messier process than necessary — if the policy ever actually had to pay out.

He isn't confused about what the new form should say. He's discussed the correct allocation with his spouse more than once, in the kind of casual, over-dinner conversation where both people nod and agree and one of them says "I'll grab the form this weekend," and then the weekend arrives and gets filled with other things, none of them more important, all of them somehow more urgent in the moment. What actually stops him, when he's honest with himself about it — and he has been honest with himself about it, more than once, usually late at night, in the specific kind of quiet reflection that produces insight without producing action — isn't the form itself. It's a small, persistent, barely-conscious worry that he'll get the specifics wrong. That he'll misjudge a percentage split, or fail to account for some tax consequence he hasn't thought of, or word something in a way that creates a different problem than the one he's trying to fix. He knows the current arrangement is wrong. But "wrong and unchanged" feels, to some quiet part of him, less risky than "changed, but maybe changed incorrectly by me, specifically, in a way I'd be responsible for."

A second scene shows the identical hesitation in a very different setting. A woman in her forties, recently promoted into a role with new stock compensation, receives clear instructions from her company's benefits team on how to elect a specific tax treatment for that compensation — a straightforward form, with a defined deadline, and a default outcome if the form isn't submitted that is, according to every piece of guidance she's read, meaningfully worse for her specific situation than the outcome the form would produce if filed correctly. She reads the instructions twice. She understands them. She even drafts the form, filling in every field, saving it as a document on her desktop titled, with a kind of gallows humor she doesn't share with anyone, "ACTUALLY SUBMIT THIS ONE." She does not submit it. The deadline passes with the default outcome taking effect automatically, and she spends a portion of an afternoon a few months later doing the math on what the correct election would have saved her — a real, specific number, attached now permanently to a decision she made not by choosing the worse outcome, but by never quite finishing the act of choosing the better one, out of a vague, hard-to-articulate fear that she'd fill something in wrong and create a different, possibly larger problem in the process of trying to fix a smaller one.

A third scene involves an older man, recently widowed, facing a decision about how to consolidate two retirement accounts — his own and a portion inherited from his late wife's — into a single, simpler structure his financial advisor has recommended clearly and repeatedly over the course of a year. He agrees, every time the topic comes up, that consolidating makes sense: fewer statements, lower combined fees, less for him to manage alone at a stage of life where managing less is exactly what he needs. And every time his advisor sends the actual paperwork required to initiate the consolidation, it sits, unsigned, for weeks, until a follow-up call prompts another round of agreement and another unsigned form. When his advisor finally asks him directly, gently, what's actually holding him back, he admits something he hadn't quite said out loud before: he's afraid that signing the wrong version of the form, or checking the wrong box on it, will somehow disrupt or diminish the portion of the money that came from his wife — that an administrative mistake on his part could, in some way he can't fully justify logically, feel like mishandling the last thing she left behind. The mechanics of the consolidation were never the actual obstacle. The much larger, much harder thing standing next to them was.

A fourth scene involves a young father who opened a custodial investment account for his daughter shortly after her birth, choosing a set of initial holdings with real, careful research at the time. Three years later, having learned considerably more about investing than he knew at the start, he's identified a lower-cost, better-structured alternative he'd choose without hesitation if he were opening the account fresh today. He hasn't switched, and the reason, when he finally names it honestly to himself, isn't about the mechanics of the switch, which his research confirms would be simple and low-risk. It's that switching would mean admitting, to himself, that his original choice — made with love, made carefully, made as one of his first real acts as a new parent — wasn't actually the best one available, and some part of him would rather quietly underperform in a decision he can still tell himself was good than actively correct it and have to sit with the small, specific admission that he could have done better the first time.

What's actually happening

The psychologists Ilana Ritov and Jonathan Baron identified and named this pattern in a series of studies beginning in 1990: omission bias — the finding that people judge harm caused by an action as worse, and more blameworthy, than equivalent or even greater harm caused by inaction, even when the two outcomes are, in every measurable respect, identical. In one of their original experiments, participants were asked to imagine a decision about whether to vaccinate a child against a disease that carried a small risk of death from the vaccine itself, alongside a larger risk of death from the disease if left unvaccinated. Even when the math clearly favored vaccination — a smaller risk from acting versus a larger risk from not acting — a significant number of participants chose not to vaccinate, and when asked to explain their reasoning, consistently expressed more concern about being the direct cause of a harm through action than about allowing a larger harm to occur through inaction. The disease outcome, if it happened, would feel like something that simply happened to the child. The vaccine outcome, if it happened, would feel like something the parent did to the child. Same child. Same outcome, mathematically speaking, weighted even more favorably toward action. Completely different emotional accounting.

This maps with almost uncomfortable precision onto the man with the beneficiary form. The current, outdated arrangement — should it ever actually pay out under its current terms — would represent a harm that simply happened, a consequence of an old form nobody updated, diffuse and impersonal in its authorship. A new form, filled out incorrectly by his own hand, would represent a harm he specifically caused, through a specific action, on a specific afternoon, with his own signature at the bottom of it. Ritov and Baron's research suggests these two outcomes don't get weighed against each other on equal terms, even though a rational assessment would treat them identically, or would in fact favor the corrected form given how clearly wrong the current arrangement is. The bias isn't really about the actual probability of making a mistake on the new form — which is, in reality, quite low, and correctable even if it happened. It's about a much older, deeper asymmetry in how the mind assigns blame: acting and getting it wrong feels like *your* failure in a way that not acting and having something go wrong simply doesn't, regardless of what the actual numbers say about which path is safer.

Ritov and Baron's later research, along with follow-up studies conducted with fellow researcher Mark Spranca and colleague Elisa Minsk in a 1991 paper, extended this finding into financial and consumer contexts specifically, and identified something important for understanding the stock compensation scene: the bias grows stronger, not weaker, as the stakes of the decision increase and as the person's uncertainty about the specific mechanics grows. The woman drafting her tax election wasn't uncertain about whether the correct election was better than the default — she was quite confident about that. She was uncertain about whether she'd filled in every field of the form correctly, and that narrower, more specific uncertainty, layered on top of a decision that already involved acting rather than simply letting a default apply, was enough to tip the outcome toward inaction, even though the default outcome was, by her own analysis, worse.

There's a related and useful distinction worth drawing here, because it clarifies exactly what omission bias is and isn't. It is not the same as simple laziness, and treating it as laziness — which is how it often gets labeled, including by the people experiencing it, who describe themselves afterward as having "just been lazy about it" — misses what's actually happening and makes the pattern harder to address. Laziness would predict avoiding effortful tasks generally, regardless of their emotional content. Omission bias is far more selective: it specifically targets tasks where an action, however small, could plausibly be blamed on the person taking it, and it leaves largely untouched tasks of equal or greater effort that don't carry that same specific liability. This is precisely why the man in this chapter's opening scene can be, and is, diligent and prompt about a wide range of other paperwork in his life — bills, renewals, routine forms with no meaningful downside risk attached to getting a detail wrong — while this one specific form sits untouched for two years. It was never about effort. It was about exposure.

There's a further piece of the mechanism worth adding, drawn from a related strand of decision research on regret: the psychologist Daniel Kahneman and his collaborators found, across a range of studies on counterfactual thinking, that people anticipate feeling more regret over a bad outcome that resulted from an unusual or non-default action than over an identical bad outcome that resulted from doing nothing or following the default path — a finding closely related to, and reinforcing, Ritov and Baron's omission-bias work. This helps explain the widower's specific fear about his late wife's money: an administrative error made through active effort to consolidate the accounts would, in his anticipation, generate a sharper, more personal, more self-directed regret than the diffuse cost of simply leaving two accounts unconsolidated indefinitely — even though the second path carries its own real costs, in fees and complexity and burden on whoever eventually has to sort out two accounts instead of one. The anticipated regret of the active mistake looms larger in imagination than the actual, accumulating cost of the passive one, and imagination, in this specific decision, is doing most of the driving.

There's a further dimension worth naming, drawn from Baron's later collaborative research examining how omission bias interacts with a person's sense of moral responsibility specifically — work suggesting that the bias intensifies when the person imagines having to explain their choice to someone else afterward. A completed form, filled in incorrectly, creates a specific, nameable moment where the person could be asked "why did you do it this way," a question with no comfortable answer if the answer is a mistake. An unfixed form, left exactly as it was, creates no equivalent moment — if it's ever questioned at all, the honest answer, "I never got around to updating it," carries a different, more diffuse, more socially forgivable quality than "I updated it and got it wrong," even though the second answer, in most of these scenarios, would have produced a meaningfully better outcome. The mind isn't just weighing outcomes here. It's weighing the story it would have to tell about how the outcome came to be, and inaction produces a far more forgivable story than action does, regardless of which one actually protects the people involved.

What it costs you

The direct financial cost varies by scenario but follows a consistent shape: a wrong or outdated arrangement, left in place because correcting it feels riskier than leaving it wrong, continues generating its own real cost the entire time it sits uncorrected — a worse tax election, higher combined fees, a beneficiary structure that would create real complications if it were ever actually triggered. None of these costs announce themselves on any given day. They accumulate silently, in exactly the same way every other pattern in this book accumulates, which is precisely why they're so easy to keep deferring.

One cost here doesn't show up in any of the other chapters quite this directly: omission bias doesn't just delay a correction — in cases involving beneficiary designations, wills, and other documents with real legal consequences, it can allow an outcome to become permanently, irreversibly locked in, in a way a rebalance or a rollover generally does not. Money sitting uninvested can still be invested next year with only the cost of the delay itself. A beneficiary form that never gets updated before the policy pays out cannot be corrected after the fact, at any price, by anyone. This raises the stakes of this particular chapter's pattern considerably higher than several of the others in this book, and it's worth sitting with that difference directly: some frozen decisions cost you money for every year they stay frozen. This one can, in the worst case, cost you the entire outcome, permanently, with no opportunity to revisit it once the triggering event has occurred.

A third cost is quieter but real: the longer a person avoids a specific form out of fear of getting it wrong, the more that specific fear generalizes into a broader, less accurate belief about their own competence with paperwork and financial administration overall — a belief that isn't actually supported by the rest of their life, where they handle comparable or more complex forms without hesitation. The man who's avoided one form for two years starts, quietly, to think of himself as someone who's "bad at this kind of thing," a self-assessment his actual track record doesn't support, but one that becomes harder to dislodge the longer this one specific avoidance continues uninterrupted.

A fourth cost applies specifically to shared or family documents, echoed in the widower's scene: an unresolved form doesn't just carry a financial or administrative cost, it carries a cost to the people who would otherwise have been protected by it, none of whom have any say in when or whether it finally gets addressed. A beneficiary designation left pointing at the wrong person doesn't only fail to serve the account holder's own wishes — it actively, if unintentionally, misdirects real money away from the people the account holder would say, if asked directly, they most wanted protected. This is a cost paid by someone other than the person doing the deferring, which is precisely what makes it so easy to keep deferring: the discomfort of fixing it lands on one person, while the eventual cost of not fixing it would land on someone else entirely, someone not in the room for any of the two years the form sat waiting.

A brief word before the overrides themselves: none of them require you to become someone who no longer feels the pull of omission bias — that pull, per Ritov and Baron's research, appears to be a stable, widely shared feature of ordinary human judgment, not a personal weakness to be argued away. The goal is narrower and more achievable: build enough structure around the specific form or document in front of you that the pull doesn't get the final say.

The overrides

Separate the fear of error from the actual error rate, explicitly. Most financial and legal forms of the kind described in this chapter are reviewed by an institution — a plan administrator, an insurer, a benefits office — before they're finalized, and most contain a built-in correction process if a mistake is caught. Before treating a form as a high-stakes, one-shot risk, find out directly, by asking, whether an error would actually be catastrophic and irreversible or whether it would simply trigger a follow-up call asking you to clarify. In the overwhelming majority of cases, it's the second. Knowing this in advance directly targets the specific anticipated-regret mechanism driving the freeze, because it shrinks the imagined downside of acting down to something closer to its real size.

The Move: fill out the form completely, save it, and set a firm, short deadline to submit it — separate from the act of filling it out. Splitting the task into two distinct steps matters more than it sounds like it should. Drafting a form carries almost none of the omission-bias weight, because a draft, sitting on a desktop, hasn't yet become an action that could be blamed on you — it's still fully reversible, still just a document. Submitting it is the actual moment the bias resists. By completing the draft first, with no pressure to submit immediately, you remove the compounding effect of two hard steps happening at once, and you give yourself a document that only requires the smaller, final act of sending it, on a date you've already committed to in advance.

Get a second set of eyes before submitting, specifically to lower the anticipated-error risk. If the fear driving the freeze is specifically about getting a detail wrong, address that fear directly rather than trying to argue yourself out of it: ask the relevant institution, an advisor, or even a knowledgeable friend to glance over the completed form before you send it. This isn't about needing permission to act — it's a concrete, practical way to shrink the actual probability of the exact mistake you're afraid of, which in turn shrinks the imagined regret that's been doing the freezing.

Reframe the current arrangement as an active choice you're making, every day it continues, rather than a neutral default. Omission bias depends on treating inaction as blame-free and action as blame-laden. You can partially dismantle this by naming the current arrangement honestly: it isn't "not yet updated." It's "the beneficiary I'm currently, actively choosing, today, by not changing it" — a sentence that, said honestly, tends to feel considerably less comfortable than the passive version, and that discomfort is useful. It restores the fact that inaction is a choice too, carrying its own consequences, rather than a safe non-choice sitting outside the decision entirely.

If the freeze involves genuine emotional weight — a late spouse's money, a family document with real history attached — name that weight directly rather than letting it hide inside a story about administrative caution. Checking the wrong box was never what the widower was actually afraid of. Honoring his wife's memory was, and once that was named plainly, in conversation with his advisor, the actual administrative fear shrank enormously, because it stopped having to carry meaning it was never built to carry. If a form feels disproportionately heavy relative to its actual content, ask directly what it's really standing in for — often it's a much larger, more legitimate feeling that deserves its own acknowledgment, separate from the paperwork.

Batch small forms together into one scheduled session, rather than facing each one as its own isolated confrontation. Omission bias tends to hit hardest when a form is encountered alone, unexpectedly, with nothing to compare it to. Grouping several small pending forms into a single, pre-scheduled hour changes the framing from "am I about to make a mistake" to "I'm doing routine paperwork maintenance" — a considerably less loaded frame that borrows some of its calm from the sheer ordinariness of batch-processing several items at once.

The Rule to Remember: A mistake you make while fixing something wrong is not worse than the wrong thing you left standing — it only feels that way because one of them has your fingerprints on it.

Chapter 4 — The Will You Haven't Written

Why Naming the Decision Makes It Harder to Face

They've talked about it in the abstract more times than either of them could count — the general shape of what should happen to the house, to the modest savings, to the two kids who are still young enough that the conversation carries a weight neither parent quite knows how to hold. They agree, broadly, on almost everything: who would raise the children if something happened to both of them, roughly how the assets should be split, the general instinct that the whole thing should be handled cleanly, without unnecessary conflict for anyone left behind to sort out. What they don't have, after six years of marriage and two children and a genuine, repeated intention to "get this done properly," is an actual will. Not a draft. Not an outline. Nothing with legal weight, nothing that would actually govern what happens if the abstract conversation ever stopped being abstract.

Every attempt to move from talking about it to actually doing it seems to run aground at the same specific point: the moment the conversation shifts from general principles to a concrete document, someone has to say, out loud, in specific and permanent language, what happens to their children if both parents die. Not as a hypothetical, softened by distance and abstraction, but as an actual clause, with actual names in it, sitting in an actual file somewhere, ready to be read by someone else on the worst day of that someone else's life. They've started the process twice — found an attorney once, filled out an online questionnaire another time — and both times, the actual drafting stalled at the exact same question, the guardian designation, and both times the stall lasted long enough that other things took priority and the whole effort quietly lost momentum, not from any disagreement about the answer, but from something neither of them has fully named: writing the answer down makes the possibility it addresses feel closer, more real, more thinkable, in a way that talking about it never quite did.

A second scene involves a single woman in her fifties, financially comfortable, with a clear and uncomplicated sense of who she'd want to inherit her estate — a niece she's close to, a few charitable causes she's supported for years, no particular complexity or conflict anywhere in the picture. She has, by her own account, "meant to get a will done" for over a decade, a phrase she's said to friends, to her accountant, to herself in her own internal narration, with a consistency that has stopped surprising anyone who knows her, including her. What she can't quite articulate, even to herself, is why a decision this uncomplicated — no dependents, no disputes, no genuinely difficult tradeoffs to weigh — has stayed unresolved for ten years. The honest answer, when she finally sits with it long enough to find it, isn't about the will's contents at all. It's that finalizing a will means sitting, deliberately, in a room, for an hour, thinking directly and specifically about her own death — not as an eventual abstraction everyone acknowledges intellectually, but as a concrete planning exercise with a signature at the bottom. Everything else in her financial life gets handled promptly and competently. This one task requires confronting something no other financial task requires confronting, and that difference, not any complexity in the actual decision, is what's kept it undone.

A third scene shows a version of this freeze that involves no death at all, useful because it demonstrates the mechanism isn't limited to mortality specifically — it applies to any decision that requires naming, concretely and specifically, an outcome the person would rather not have to look directly at. A man in his late thirties, recently diagnosed with a manageable but chronic health condition, has been told clearly by his doctor and financial advisor alike that he should update his disability insurance coverage, since his current policy — purchased years earlier, before the diagnosis — no longer adequately reflects his actual risk profile or his family's needs if his condition were to worsen and limit his ability to work. He agrees entirely with the recommendation. He has not made the call to initiate the update, for reasons he's only partly aware of: doing so requires filling out a new application that asks him to describe, in specific written detail, exactly how his condition might progress and exactly what that progression would mean for his ability to earn income — a document that would force him to sit with and articulate a version of his own future he's been managing, quite successfully in every other part of his life, by simply not looking at it too directly.

A fourth scene involves a woman in her early forties, recently separated, working through the process of updating her estate documents to reflect her new circumstances — removing her former spouse as a decision-maker, naming a new set of instructions for her own care should she ever be unable to make decisions for herself. Every other piece of the separation has moved forward with real, visible progress: the shared finances have been untangled, the living arrangements settled, the practical logistics handled with a competence that's surprised even her. This one document sits apart from all of it, not because it's legally complicated — her attorney has told her plainly it's a short, straightforward update — but because completing it requires her to sit, alone, with the specific and unwelcome thought of being incapacitated with no one by her side who used to be that person by default. The document isn't hard. Being the one required to name, in writing, who takes that role now is.

What's actually happening

The economist George Loewenstein, working with colleagues Elke Weber, Christopher Hsee, and Ned Welch in an influential 2001 paper titled "Risk as Feelings," documented something that ran against the traditional assumption, common in earlier economic models, that people make decisions by calculating expected outcomes and weighing them rationally. Loewenstein and his co-authors found instead that anticipated feelings — the emotional forecast of how a decision or its possible outcomes would feel, not the actual probability-weighted math of those outcomes — frequently drive behavior more powerfully than the calculated risk itself. This matters enormously for a decision like a will, because the actual probability of the guardianship clause ever being invoked is, for most families, extremely low. But the *feeling* of writing that clause — the vivid, specific, emotionally loaded act of naming who would raise your children in your absence — registers with an intensity wildly disproportionate to the statistical likelihood of the event it describes, and that intensity, per Loewenstein's research, is often what actually governs whether the decision gets made at all.

This is worth sitting with directly, because it explains something that otherwise looks contradictory: two parents who are, by any reasonable measure, careful and responsible people, capable of making dozens of other consequential financial decisions without hesitation, freeze specifically and only at this one clause. It isn't that the decision is objectively harder than their other financial choices — determining a guardian, once the actual candidates are considered, is often a relatively short and clear conversation. It's that writing it down requires generating, briefly but vividly, the emotional experience of imagining both parents gone, and that imagined emotional experience, per Loewenstein's research, exerts a pull on behavior that has almost nothing to do with how statistically unlikely the actual scenario is.

There's a closely related concept worth introducing here, drawn from a substantial body of research on mortality salience — the effect of being made to consciously confront one's own eventual death — most extensively developed within terror management theory, a framework built initially by social psychologists Jeff Greenberg, Sheldon Solomon, and Tom Pyszczynski beginning in 1986. Their research, replicated across a large number of studies, found that direct, explicit reminders of one's own mortality reliably produce measurable psychological responses — increased anxiety, avoidance behavior, and a strong, largely unconscious motivation to disengage from whatever specific task triggered the reminder, in favor of activities that restore a sense of psychological distance from the topic. A will is, among the ordinary documents of adult financial life, one of the very few that requires this kind of direct confrontation as a structural feature of the task itself — you cannot draft a will without, at some point, explicitly considering your own death as a concrete planning premise, in a way that a rebalance or a rollover simply never requires. This is precisely why the woman in her fifties can competently handle every other item on her financial to-do list while this single one sits untouched for a decade: it isn't a harder decision. It's the only decision on her list that structurally requires mortality salience as a prerequisite to completing it.

The disability insurance scene extends this same mechanism into adjacent territory, worth naming distinctly: the anticipated feeling driving the man's avoidance isn't about death specifically, but about articulating, in concrete written language, a future version of himself defined by decline — a task that requires the identical kind of direct, unavoidable confrontation with an unwanted possibility that a will requires with mortality.

Loewenstein's broader "risk as feelings" framework applies just as cleanly here: the actual probability of his condition significantly worsening may be genuinely low, and the coverage update genuinely modest in cost and complexity. What's driving the freeze isn't the math. It's the vivid, specific emotional weight of the exercise required to complete the paperwork correctly, which asks him to imagine, in detail, precisely the outcome he'd most like to not imagine.

There's a further piece of research worth adding, from the psychologists Terry Connolly and Marcel Zeelenberg, whose work on regret theory examined how people specifically anticipate and try to avoid decisions that would require them to directly confront an uncomfortable counterfactual. Their research found that people will frequently choose to delay a decision indefinitely — even a decision with a clearly correct answer — specifically to avoid the discrete, nameable moment where the decision has to be committed to, because commitment itself, separate from the decision's actual content, carries its own emotional cost. This distinguishes the pattern in this chapter from the status quo bias covered in Chapter 1 in an important way: it isn't only that staying still feels safer than the general risk of choosing wrong. It's that some decisions specifically require a moment of vivid, explicit confrontation with something painful to think about, and avoiding that specific moment, not the decision's broader outcome, is what's actually being protected.

There's a further piece of terror management research worth adding, because it explains why this specific freeze so often survives even genuine, repeated intention to resolve it. Studies conducted within the terror management framework have found that avoidance in response to mortality salience isn't limited to avoiding the triggering topic itself — it frequently generalizes into avoiding an entire cluster of adjacent tasks that share even a loose association with the original trigger. This is worth naming plainly for the couple in this chapter's opening scene: it isn't only the will that's stalled. Related tasks — updating life insurance beneficiaries, finalizing a healthcare proxy, even routine estate-planning conversations with parents about their own wishes — tend to cluster together and stall together, not because any of them individually carries the same emotional weight as the will's central clause, but because proximity to the topic is often enough to trigger the same avoidance response by association. Addressing the will in isolation, without recognizing this clustering, frequently leaves the surrounding tasks just as frozen as they were before, waiting for their own turn to be named directly.

What it costs you

The most serious cost in this chapter is different in kind from most of the others in this book, and worth naming without softening it: an unwritten will doesn't just cost money or efficiency – in the specific, worst-case scenario it's meant to address, it hands the actual decisions to a default legal process that may bear little resemblance to what either parent would have chosen, at exactly the moment when the people affected are least equipped to navigate an unclear or contested outcome. This isn't a cost that compounds gradually and reveals itself eventually, the way most of this book's patterns work. It's a cost that either never materializes at all, or materializes completely, with no partial version and no opportunity for a later correction.

A second, more common cost applies regardless of whether the worst-case scenario ever occurs: the ongoing, low-grade psychological weight of an unresolved task this significant doesn't sit quietly in the background the way a deferred rebalance does. Both parents in the first scene report, separately, a recurring, free-floating unease specifically tied to the will — not constant, but reliably triggered by certain moments (a plane trip together without the kids, a news story about a family tragedy) that surface the exact anticipated feeling the avoidance was built to manage. Avoiding the task doesn't eliminate the feeling it was meant to protect against. It just relocates that feeling from a single, contained hour of drafting into a recurring, unpredictable background presence that shows up on its own schedule instead of theirs.

There's a third cost specific to the disability insurance scene worth naming: coverage gaps, unlike most financial gaps, often can't be closed retroactively once a condition has progressed — insurers frequently exclude or heavily price coverage for conditions already diagnosed or worsened by the time an application is finally submitted. Every additional month of delay here isn't neutral the way a delayed rollover is neutral, recoverable in full the moment action finally happens. It's a window that can narrow or close entirely, quietly, without any specific moment announcing that it's happened.

A fourth cost is a direct consequence of the clustering effect described above: because avoidance around one mortality-linked task tends to spread to adjacent ones, a family that's deferred a will often discovers, when the topic finally does get addressed, that several other related gaps have been quietly accumulating alongside it the entire time — an outdated healthcare directive, an unnamed emergency contact, a life insurance policy nobody's reviewed since the youngest child was born. None of these were separately, consciously avoided. They were swept up in the same general current, and the eventual reckoning, when it finally comes, is almost always larger than the single document that originally seemed to be the only thing pending.

The overrides

Separate the emotionally loaded clause from the rest of the document, and do the easy parts first. Loewenstein's research suggests the freeze attaches to the specific moment of vivid emotional confrontation, not to the task as a whole. Draft everything else in the document first — asset distribution, executor designation, the more mechanical sections — and treat the emotionally loaded clause (guardianship, specific mortality-framed language) as its own separate, final step, scheduled deliberately rather than encountered by surprise partway through. Momentum built on the easier sections makes the harder one measurably less likely to stall the entire project.

The Move: write the hardest sentence first, roughly, in private, with no legal weight attached, before you ever sit down with an attorney. Take out a piece of paper, alone, and write the actual guardian names, or the actual outcome you're avoiding articulating, in plain, informal language — not the final legal wording, just the honest, rough version. This decouples the emotional confrontation from the formal, permanent-feeling act of signing a legal document, letting you face the hard part once, privately, at your own pace, so that the actual drafting session with a professional becomes a matter of formalizing a decision you've already made rather than making it live, under pressure, in front of someone else.

Give the mortality-salience response a fixed time box, and expect it, rather than treating it as a sign to stop. Knowing in advance that this specific task will produce a genuine, uncomfortable emotional response — not a sign that something's wrong with the process, but an expected and well-documented feature of exactly this kind of decision — makes the response easier to sit through without retreating. Set aside a specific, limited window (forty-five minutes, say) for the hardest part specifically, and treat finishing that window, regardless of how it felt, as success, rather than waiting to feel emotionally ready before starting.

Use a professional specifically to absorb the moment of commitment. Loewenstein and Connolly's research both point to the moment of committing to a decision, not just its content, as a distinct source of avoidance. An attorney, an advisor, or even a structured online service that walks you through the questions in sequence provides an external structure that carries you through the commitment moment rather than requiring you to generate it entirely on your own, in the same way a scheduled appointment with a dentist gets a checkup done that pure intention never quite manages alone.

Reframe the document as protection for the people you love, not a rehearsal of losing them. The emotional framing of the task matters more than it sounds like it should. A will drafted while dwelling on the triggering scenario feels unbearable. The identical document, reframed explicitly as "the specific, concrete way I make sure the people I love are taken care of, regardless of what happens to me," shifts the emotional center of the task from the feared outcome to the love driving the precaution — the same information, organized around a different feeling entirely.

Address the whole cluster deliberately, once you've named it, rather than letting adjacent tasks keep hiding behind the one you finally finished. Since mortality-linked avoidance tends to spread across several related documents at once, don't stop at the single task that prompted this chapter's recognition. List every other item likely swept into the same avoidance — the healthcare directive, the outdated beneficiary form, the emergency contact nobody's updated in a decade — and schedule each one individually, using the same time-boxed approach, before the cluster has a chance to quietly reform around whatever's left unaddressed.

The Rule to Remember: The document was never really about your death — it was about the people left standing afterward, and they deserve more than your discomfort writing it down.

Chapter 5 — The Rebalance You Keep Postponing

Why the Default Always Wins

The allocation was correct once, carefully chosen, actually researched — he remembers the specific evening he built it, sitting at his kitchen table with three browser tabs open, cross-referencing recommendations, landing on a mix he felt genuinely good about at the time: a specific split between stocks and bonds, calibrated to a retirement date roughly twenty-five years out, exactly the kind of deliberate, informed decision this book keeps insisting people are capable of making when they actually sit down to make one. That was six years ago. In the time since, the market has moved in the way markets move — unevenly, with stretches of strong growth in some parts of the portfolio and slower growth in others — and the careful allocation from that kitchen-table evening has drifted, gradually and invisibly, into something meaningfully different from what he originally chose: more concentrated in growth-oriented holdings than he'd intended, less balanced than the plan called for, simply because nobody adjusted it as the pieces moved at different speeds.

He knows this. He's known it for at least two of those six years, since a casual conversation with a coworker who happened to mention rebalancing her own accounts and asked, in passing, when he'd last done the same to his. He'd genuinely not known the answer off the top of his head, which struck him, at the time, as slightly alarming — enough that he opened his account that same evening and did the actual math, confirming the drift was real and meaningfully larger than he would have guessed. He set a reminder on his phone for the following month. That reminder has since been dismissed, rescheduled, and dismissed again, close to a dozen times now, each time with the same brief flicker of intention followed by the same quiet decision that this particular evening isn't the right one, that next week will be better, that the account isn't in any immediate danger from waiting a little longer.

A second scene shows a version of the same drift playing out for a couple managing a joint account together, useful because it demonstrates how the freeze survives even active, ongoing attention to the account. They check the account regularly —

genuinely regularly, logging in together most months to look at the overall balance and feel a reasonable, warranted satisfaction at its steady growth. What they don't do, despite checking the total often, is look underneath the total at the actual composition of what's driving it, and so the same drift that affected the man in the first scene has been happening to them too, unnoticed specifically because the number they're watching — the overall balance — keeps looking fine, growing steadily, giving them no visible signal that anything underneath it needs attention. The account isn't neglected in any way either of them would recognize as neglect. It's watched constantly, at exactly the wrong level of detail to catch the specific thing that actually needs adjusting.

A third scene involves a small business owner managing her own retirement account alongside her company's finances, someone whose professional life revolves entirely around noticing and correcting exactly this kind of drift in other contexts — she rebalances her business's inventory, her cash flow projections, her staffing levels, constantly and skillfully, treating drift as a routine, expected part of running anything over time. Her personal retirement account, chosen and funded years ago through her business's benefits structure, has never received the same treatment, not because she lacks the skill to apply it, but because the account exists slightly outside the daily operational rhythm that makes her so effective at catching drift everywhere else in her business — it isn't a line item she reviews weekly, it's a thing that exists in the background, on autopilot, and autopilot, once established, tends to stay exactly as it was set, regardless of how skilled the person flying the plane happens to be at everything else they do.

A fourth scene involves a man who inherited a modest investment account from a parent several years ago, along with the specific allocation his parent had chosen decades earlier — a mix that made sense for an investor in his parent's stage of life and circumstances, and that has never once been reviewed against his own, considerably different situation since the account passed to him. He hasn't touched it, not out of any active decision to preserve his parent's choices as a kind of memorial, though that's the explanation he reaches for when asked, but because reviewing it honestly would mean acknowledging that his own needs are genuinely different from the needs that produced the original allocation — a small, quiet act of separation from a parent he still misses, disguised as simple inertia. The account has drifted further from any sensible target for him specifically with every year it's gone unexamined, carrying a mix of tax and estate considerations neither he nor his parent's original allocation ever anticipated.

What's actually happening

The economists Eric Johnson and Daniel Goldstein published a widely cited study in 2003, in the journal *Science*, examining organ donation registration rates across several European countries — a study that, on its surface, has nothing to do with retirement accounts, and that turns out to explain the rebalancing freeze with remarkable precision. Johnson and Goldstein found an enormous difference in organ donor participation rates between countries that used an opt-in system, where citizens had to actively register to become donors, and countries that used an opt-out system, where citizens were automatically registered unless they actively withdrew — a difference not of a few percentage points, but of tens of percentage points, driven by nothing other than which behavior required active effort and which one didn't. The underlying preferences of the citizens in question, as best as could be measured, didn't differ meaningfully between countries. What differed was the default, and the default, Johnson and Goldstein's research made clear, exerts an influence on real, consequential behavior that dwarfs almost every other factor typically assumed to matter more — including factors like religious belief, political affiliation, or stated personal values, all of which showed far weaker correlation with actual donor status than the simple structural question of which behavior required a form.

Applied to the rebalancing decision, the mechanism is direct: once an allocation is set, "leave it as it currently sits" becomes the default, requiring zero action, while "adjust it back to the original plan" requires an active, deliberate step — logging in, calculating the current drift, executing specific trades or transfers. Johnson and Goldstein's research suggests this asymmetry alone, entirely independent of how much anyone actually values the outcome of rebalancing, is enough to explain why the correction keeps not happening, month after month, dismissed reminder after dismissed reminder. The man in the first scene isn't failing to rebalance because he doesn't understand the value of doing so — he clearly does, he did the math, he confirmed the drift was real. He's failing to rebalance because the corrected allocation has never once been the default option presented to him. It has always required an active opt-in, and active opt-ins, per Johnson and Goldstein's findings, lose to passive defaults with startling, consistent regularity, regardless of the stakes involved or the sophistication of the person facing the choice.

There's a related and important extension of this research worth bringing in here, from behavioral economists Richard Thaler and Shlomo Benartzi, whose influential work on retirement savings, published in a 2004 paper titled "Save More Tomorrow," applied default-effect logic directly to the problem of chronically low retirement contribution rates. Rather than simply asking employees to increase their contributions — a request that, per the same status quo dynamics covered in Chapter 1, reliably produced little change — Thaler and

Benartzi designed a program that pre-committed employees, with their advance consent, to automatic future contribution increases timed to coincide with future pay raises, unless the employee actively opted out. Participation and average savings rates rose substantially under this structure, not because employees' underlying desire to save more had changed, but because the researchers had, in effect, engineered the correct behavior to become the new default, requiring active effort only to avoid it rather than to achieve it. Their broader finding — that people will accept and even benefit from a beneficial default they would never have actively chosen to initiate themselves — points directly toward the most effective override for the rebalancing freeze specifically: the goal isn't to generate more willpower to overcome the default. It's to restructure which option gets to be the default in the first place.

It's worth being precise about why the second scene — the couple who check regularly but never at the right level of detail — represents a distinct variant of this same mechanism worth naming separately. Their freeze isn't purely about effort avoidance; it's compounded by what researchers studying attention and default behavior sometimes call the wrong salience target. The overall balance, growing steadily, is highly visible and continuously reinforced as "the thing to watch," while the underlying composition — the actual driver of long-term risk and return — sits one layer beneath the visible number, effectively invisible to a monitoring routine calibrated to check the wrong metric. This is a version of the default effect operating on attention itself rather than on action: the default thing to look at, once established, becomes as sticky and as resistant to change as the default thing to do.

There's a further wrinkle worth adding from Johnson and Goldstein's own later research extending their original organ-donation findings into other financial and consumer domains: they found the default effect grows especially powerful specifically in decisions framed as maintaining rather than changing a *complex* prior arrangement — precisely the shape of a portfolio's asset allocation, which involves multiple moving pieces (stocks, bonds, sometimes several sub-categories of each) rather than a single simple setting. A decision with only one dimension to reconsider, their follow-up work suggests, is more likely to eventually get revisited than a decision with several interdependent dimensions, because reconsidering a multi-part arrangement requires reconstructing the entire original reasoning, not just flipping a single switch. This is worth sitting with directly: the six-year-old allocation isn't resistant to correction merely because correcting it requires effort. It's resistant because correcting it requires effort *proportional to its own complexity*, and a portfolio built with real care, across several categories, is by that same virtue harder to revisit casually than a simpler decision would be — the very thoughtfulness that went into building it well the first time is part of what makes it so easy to leave untouched afterward.

What it costs you

The financial cost of unaddressed drift compounds specifically because the direction of drift, left unattended for long enough, tends to reduce diversification exactly when diversification matters most — an allocation that's grown more concentrated than intended carries more risk than the plan called for, often without the person holding it having any clear sense that their actual risk exposure no longer matches their actual risk tolerance. This mismatch doesn't announce itself gradually, the way a fee gap does. It sits invisible, exactly as risky as it's become, until a downturn arrives and reveals a portfolio meaningfully less protected than its owner believed it to be — a discovery made at precisely the worst possible moment to be making it.

A second cost follows directly from the couple's scene: monitoring the wrong metric doesn't just fail to catch drift — it actively produces false confidence, which is arguably worse than no monitoring at all. A person who never checks their account at least knows they don't know their current allocation. A couple who check regularly, see a healthy, growing balance, and conclude everything is fine has replaced genuine uncertainty with a specific, false certainty that the account is being properly managed, a belief that will hold right up until the exact moment it's tested by conditions the drifted allocation was never actually built to withstand.

A third cost echoes a theme from earlier chapters, worth restating in this specific context: every dismissed reminder trains the next reminder to be a little easier to dismiss. The man's roughly-dozen dismissed rebalancing prompts haven't been neutral events. Each one has been a small, repeated rehearsal of "not now," strengthening exactly the pattern that keeps producing the drift he already knows about and has already, once, confirmed with real numbers.

A fourth cost is specific to the compounding complexity described above: the longer a multi-part allocation goes unrebalanced, the more the eventual correction itself grows in scope and difficulty, since drift doesn't stay confined to one category — it typically widens across several simultaneously, each one requiring its own specific adjustment by the time anyone finally sits down to fix it. A rebalance deferred for six months might involve two or three modest trades. The identical rebalance deferred for six years, as in this chapter's opening scene, often involves a far larger, more consequential reshuffling, executed all at once, at a moment the market happens to choose rather than one the account holder does — precisely the kind of large, high-stakes, single-sitting task this book has repeatedly shown gets deferred more easily than a small, incremental one ever would.

One further note before the overrides: the goal of every technique below is the same one Johnson and Goldstein's research points to directly — change which behavior is the default, not how much willpower you bring to the task. A person who tries to solve this chapter's pattern through sheer resolve is fighting a structural force with a psychological tool, a mismatch this book has shown, chapter after chapter, rarely ends well.

The overrides

Automate the correction itself, not just the reminder to perform it. Most major brokerages and retirement plan providers now offer automatic rebalancing as a selectable feature — a setting, usually buried a few menus deep, that will periodically and automatically return an account to its target allocation without requiring an active step each time. Turning this on, once, converts the entire chapter's mechanism from working against you to working for you: per Johnson and Goldstein's core finding, whichever behavior requires no ongoing action becomes the one that actually happens, so the goal is to make "stay correctly balanced" the thing that requires zero effort, rather than "drift further" being the thing that requires zero effort.

The Move: if automatic rebalancing isn't available, build a Thaler-and-Benartzi-style pre-commitment instead. Schedule a specific, recurring calendar appointment — annually is sufficient for most accounts — and, critically, commit in advance, in writing, to a specific action you'll take at that appointment regardless of how you feel about it in the moment: "every January 15th, I rebalance back to my original targets, no exceptions, no reassessment of whether it's a good time." The Save More Tomorrow research succeeded specifically because the commitment was made in advance, at a calm moment, and then executed automatically later — not because anyone found a way to simply want it more in the moment it counted.

Realign what you monitor, not just how often you monitor it. If your regular check-ins are tracking the overall balance rather than the underlying allocation, deliberately change what the check-in is actually for. Replace "log in and look at the total" with "log in and compare the current allocation percentages to the original target percentages" — a small shift in what the habit is actually checking, but one that directly targets the wrong-salience-target problem the couple's scene demonstrates.

Set a drift threshold, in writing, that triggers action automatically rather than requiring a fresh judgment call each time. Decide in advance — five percentage points off target is a reasonable standard many advisors use — the specific amount of drift that will trigger a rebalance, and commit that when your regular check reveals drift past that threshold, the rebalance happens that same week, not "soon." A pre-set threshold removes the need to decide, in the moment, whether this particular instance of drift is worth acting on — a decision that, per Chapter 1's status quo research, the current arrangement will otherwise reliably win.

Treat the professional skill you already have in another domain as evidence you're capable of this one, not as an argument that you should already be doing it without help. The business owner in this chapter's third scene is skilled at catching drift everywhere except her own retirement account — not because the account is uniquely difficult, but because it sits outside her normal operational rhythm. The fix isn't more self-discipline. It's deliberately importing the account into a rhythm she already trusts, the same weekly or monthly review structure she already uses for everything else she manages well.

Simplify the underlying structure itself, if complexity is what's making rebalancing feel too effortful to face. If the multi-part-complexity cost described above is what's actually driving the freeze, consider whether the portfolio needs quite as many separate moving pieces as it currently has. A simpler structure, built from a smaller number of broader holdings, is easier to monitor honestly and easier to correct quickly, and the modest cost of simplifying is often far smaller than the compounding cost of a complex structure nobody ever quite gets around to maintaining properly.

The Rule to Remember: The allocation you built once was correct for one afternoon — staying that way forever was never going to happen on its own, and it was never supposed to have to.

Chapter 6 — The Conversation You Keep Rescheduling

Why an Open Decision Never Closes Itself

It comes up almost every time they're driving somewhere together, which is a specific, recognizable pattern once you notice it — the conversation about consolidating their finances, six years into a marriage that's kept two entirely separate banking systems running in parallel since before the wedding, seems to only ever surface in the fifteen or twenty minutes of unstructured time a car ride provides, and it never once, in six years, has made it past the first few sentences before one of them changes the subject, gently, to something the drive has conveniently produced — a billboard, a song, the exit coming up. Neither of them has ever said, directly, that they don't want to have the conversation. Both of them, separately, if you asked them privately, would tell you they know it needs to happen and that they intend to actually sit down and have it properly, soon, once things settle down a little.

Things have not settled down, in six years, in the specific way that would apparently be required for this conversation to happen on purpose rather than by accident in a moving car. What's notable, looking at the pattern honestly, isn't that they lack the time — a real, deliberate version of this conversation would take perhaps ninety minutes, and they've had ninety free minutes together dozens of times across six years without ever once using them for this. What's happening instead is something closer to what one of them, prompted eventually to describe it, calls "the conversation that's always fifteen minutes long and never gets anywhere" — a conversation that opens the same handful of times a year, gets partway through the same handful of initial points, and then closes again without resolution, only to reopen, identically, a few months later, having made no net progress in either direction. It isn't avoided entirely. It's revisited constantly, which somehow produces the same practical result as avoiding it, while feeling, from the inside, like active engagement rather than deferral.

A second scene shows a similar pattern between two adult siblings jointly responsible for managing their aging mother's finances, a task that requires the two of them to agree on a specific set of decisions — power of attorney designation, a plan for her long-term care costs, an updated understanding of her actual asset picture — that neither sibling wants to be the one to force into a formal decision, given how loaded the underlying subject is. They talk about it after nearly every visit to their mother's house, in the parking lot afterward, in a pattern that's become so routine neither of them notices it as a pattern anymore: a real, substantive conversation that covers real ground, followed by "we really need to get this on paper," followed by nothing on paper, followed by the identical conversation, in the identical parking lot, three or four months later. The subject stays perpetually open. It never fully closes into an actual, executed decision, because closing it would require one of them to take the concrete first step — scheduling the attorney appointment, drafting the actual document — and each parking-lot conversation ends with a vague, unassigned sense that "we'll figure out next steps," a sentence that has never once, across more than a dozen repetitions, produced an actual next step.

A third scene involves two business partners who've discussed, repeatedly and in real depth, restructuring their profit-sharing arrangement to better reflect how their respective contributions to the business have shifted over the past several years — one partner now handling significantly more of the operational load than the original fifty-fifty split anticipated when the business began. Both partners agree, in every conversation, that the current split no longer reflects reality fairly. Neither has drafted a specific new proposal, because doing so would require one of them to name an actual number, and naming an actual number turns an abstract, comfortable agreement that "something should probably change" into a concrete, specific ask that the other partner might, for the first time, actually disagree with. The conversation stays open, revisited every few months over the same lunch, precisely because staying open avoids the risk of a real number producing a real conflict — even though both partners privately suspect, correctly, that the eventual real number will be close enough to what each of them already expects that the imagined conflict is considerably larger than the actual one would likely be.

A fourth scene involves two adult siblings, on the opposite end of a related situation, dividing responsibility for a parent's household expenses after that parent has moved in with one of them following a health decline. Both agree, in principle, that the sibling providing daily care should be compensated somehow for the disproportionate burden — in money, in a larger eventual share of an inheritance, in something concrete — and both have raised the topic, gently, more than once, always in the same careful, conflict-averse register neither wants to push past. Eighteen months into the new living arrangement, no actual agreement exists, written or otherwise, and the sibling providing daily care has begun keeping a private, informal log of expenses and hours, not because she plans to present it as a demand, but because some part of her recognizes that an unresolved understanding this significant, allowed to drift long enough, has a way of eventually surfacing as resentment rather than as the calm, fair conversation both of them originally intended to have.

What's actually happening

The organizational psychologist Piers Steel conducted an extensive meta-analysis of procrastination research, published in 2007, synthessizing several decades of prior studies into what he called the temporal motivation theory of procrastination — a framework describing how the motivation to complete a task is influenced not just by how much a person values the outcome, but by how far away in time the task's deadline or consequence sits, and critically, by how much genuine uncertainty and discomfort the task itself involves. Steel's research found that tasks combining high uncertainty, high discomfort, and no hard external deadline are disproportionately likely to be chronically deferred, regardless of how much the person genuinely values completing them — and a shared financial conversation with real emotional stakes and no forced deadline fits this profile with unusual precision. Nobody is requiring the couple to consolidate their accounts by a specific date. Nobody is requiring the siblings to finalize the power-of-attorney arrangement by a specific date. In the absence of an externally imposed deadline, Steel's research suggests, these conversations remain permanently available to be deferred, because there is never a specific moment where deferring them further carries an immediate, visible cost.

There's a particular feature of this chapter's pattern that distinguishes it from simple procrastination, though, and it's worth naming precisely, because it explains why these conversations keep reopening rather than staying closed the way a fully avoided task would. The psychologist Bluma Zeigarnik, working in the 1920s, identified what's now called the Zeigarnik effect: the finding that incomplete or interrupted tasks are remembered significantly better, and intrude on conscious attention significantly more, than completed tasks. An open, unresolved question doesn't fade quietly into the background the way a fully forgotten task might. It keeps surfacing, precisely because it's unfinished, precisely because some part of the mind treats an open loop as something requiring ongoing tracking. This explains why the conversation reliably surfaces on every long car ride, every post-visit parking lot conversation, every recurring lunch — the Zeigarnik effect keeps the topic actively present in a way a truly forgotten task never would be, while Steel's temporal motivation research explains why that constant presence never actually converts into resolution. The topic is too psychologically "loud" to fully drop, and too structurally deadline-free to ever fully close. It's trapped in a kind of permanent middle state — neither dismissed nor resolved — that both couples and business partners in these scenes describe, independently, using nearly the same phrase: "we keep meaning to actually sit down and finish this."

There's a further layer worth adding, specific to shared decisions rather than individual ones, drawn from research on group decision-making and diffusion of responsibility, a concept most closely associated with social psychologists Bibb Latané and John Darley, whose foundational studies in the late 1960s examined why individuals in a group are often less likely to take responsibility for addressing a problem than a single individual acting alone — not from indifference, but from an unconscious, largely automatic assumption that responsibility, when shared among multiple people, becomes correspondingly diluted for each individual person involved. Applied to the parking-lot conversation between siblings, or the recurring lunch between business partners: each person in the conversation experiences the topic as genuinely important and genuinely intends to move it forward, but each also, quietly, assumes the *next* concrete step is at least partly the other person's to take, and that mutual, largely unconscious assumption is enough, repeated across a dozen conversations, to keep a topic both parties genuinely care about permanently short of resolution.

It's worth naming precisely why the business-partners scene carries an additional layer the other two don't: the specific fear of naming a number and discovering real disagreement. This connects back to the anticipated-regret research introduced in Chapter 4 — the imagined conflict that would follow a concrete, specific proposal looms larger in the partners' minds than the actual, statistically likely outcome, which, per their own private estimates, would probably land close to what both already expect. Keeping the conversation abstract protects against a conflict that exists mostly in anticipation, at the direct cost of ever reaching the resolution both partners say, consistently and sincerely, that they want.

There's a final layer worth adding, drawn from Steel's broader meta-analysis and worth naming specifically because it applies to every scene in this chapter: Steel's research found that procrastination on any given task correlates strongly with how far removed the task's consequence feels in time, even when the actual consequence, once it eventually arrives, is severe. A car ride, a parking lot, a recurring lunch — none of these settings carry any felt urgency, because the actual triggering event each conversation is meant to prepare for (a shared financial emergency, a parent's health crisis, a partnership dispute) feels comfortably distant on any given ordinary day. This is precisely what makes shared, undeadlined conversations so much more durable a freeze than individual, deadline-bound tasks: there's no equivalent of a due date quietly applying pressure in the background. The pressure, when it finally does arrive, arrives all at once, in the form of the exact event the conversation was supposed to have already addressed.

What it costs you

The direct cost varies by scenario, but shares a consistent shape: every month a shared financial decision stays open rather than resolved is a month the underlying arrangement — separate accounts that could be more efficiently managed together, an unclear power-of-attorney situation that would create real complications in an emergency, a profit split that no longer reflects actual contribution — continues operating exactly as it currently does, generating whatever specific cost that arrangement generates, uninterrupted by the dozen well-intentioned conversations that have, so far, produced no actual change to it.

There's a cost specific to the Zeigarnik-effect dynamic worth naming directly: an open loop that keeps resurfacing without ever closing carries its own real psychological weight, distinct from and additional to the underlying financial cost. Each of these people reports, independently, a low background awareness of the unresolved topic — not constant distress, but a recurring, mildly unpleasant sense of an unfinished obligation, triggered by car rides, by visits to an aging parent, by a recurring lunch that's stopped feeling entirely comfortable. This is a cost the fully avoided task in Chapter 3 doesn't carry in quite the same way — a form sitting silently in a drawer, unopened, doesn't intrude on daily attention the way a topic that gets actively, repeatedly reopened and then abandoned does. Perversely, the very fact that these people keep trying to address the issue is part of what keeps it psychologically present and unresolved.

A third cost is specific to the siblings' scene: decisions with real time sensitivity — an aging parent's care arrangements chief among them — don't wait for the conversation to eventually resolve itself on its own schedule. A power-of-attorney designation left unresolved doesn't just sit neutrally until the siblings finally get around to it. It leaves a genuine gap, exposed and unaddressed, for exactly the length of time the parking-lot conversation keeps reopening without closing — a gap that becomes acutely, urgently visible only in the exact kind of emergency it was meant to prepare for, at precisely the moment when there's no longer any time left to close it calmly.

It's worth being specific about what "calmly" is actually protecting, because it explains why the parking-lot version of this conversation, however imperfect, is still worth more than the emergency-room version everyone is unconsciously risking by continuing to defer it. A power-of-attorney conversation had on a quiet Sunday allows for genuine deliberation — comparing options, consulting an attorney, taking a week to reconsider a detail that feels wrong on first read. The identical conversation, forced by a sudden hospitalization or a diagnosis, allows for none of that. It happens in a hallway, under real time pressure, often with genuine disagreement between family members who no longer have the luxury of resolving that disagreement slowly. The siblings aren't just risking a gap in coverage. They're trading a calm, correctable process for a rushed, largely uncorrectable one, and the trade is happening by default, one deferred parking-lot conversation at a time, without either of them ever having consciously agreed to make it.

A fourth cost is easy to miss because it doesn't show up in either person's finances directly: a topic that keeps reopening without resolving tends to slowly erode each person's confidence not just in the decision itself, but in the relationship's ability to actually finish things together. The couple who can't get past the first few sentences of the same conversation for six years, the siblings whose parking-lot talks never produce a next step, the partners who keep circling the same lunch — each repetition is quietly teaching everyone involved that this particular subject, and by extension this particular working relationship, doesn't reliably convert good intentions into resolution. That's a heavier cost than the underlying financial question itself, because it doesn't stay contained to one topic. It becomes evidence, however unfairly, about the partnership generally.

Before the overrides, it's worth being honest about a specific trap: reading this chapter and resolving, in the moment, to "finally have the real conversation soon" is precisely the goal-intention pattern that's kept the conversation unresolved for years already. What follows is designed to convert that resolve into something more specific before the feeling of resolve has a chance to fade the way it always has before.

The overrides

Give the conversation an actual deadline, external to the conversation itself. Steel's temporal motivation research points directly at the fix: tasks without a hard deadline get deferred indefinitely, so manufacture one. Schedule a specific date and time for the full, real version of the conversation — not "sometime soon," an actual date on a shared calendar, treated with the same seriousness as an appointment with an outside professional, ideally with an actual outside professional or a specific location involved (an attorney's office, a scheduled call with an advisor) that makes rescheduling carry a real, visible cost rather than none at all.

The Move: end every partial conversation with one written, assigned next step before it closes, not a vague shared intention. The pattern in every scene in this chapter is a conversation that opens repeatedly and closes with nothing concrete attached to it. Break that specific pattern directly: the next time the topic comes up, however briefly, do not let it end without both people agreeing, out loud, on one specific, small, assigned action — "I will call the attorney's office by Friday" — attached to one specific person's name. This doesn't require finishing the whole conversation. It requires converting whatever partial progress does happen into a discrete, ownable task rather than letting it dissolve back into the open loop the Zeigarnik effect keeps resurfacing without resolving.

Name the diffusion of responsibility directly, out loud, to counteract it. Latané and Darley's research suggests the diffusion happens automatically and largely outside conscious awareness — which means naming it consciously is itself a partial fix. Say, plainly, in the conversation: "I think we've both been assuming the other person would take the next step, and neither of us has." This single sentence, spoken honestly, tends to break the pattern more effectively than another round of the conversation itself, because it makes visible a dynamic that was previously operating silently.

If fear of conflict is part of what's keeping the topic abstract, request the specific number or proposal in writing, privately, before the shared conversation happens. The business partners' scene benefits from a version of Chapter 4's override: do the emotionally loaded part alone first. Ask each partner to independently draft their own proposed number, privately, before the next lunch, so the shared conversation becomes a matter of comparing two already-formed positions — usually closer together than either partner feared — rather than requiring someone to generate and voice the first number live, under direct social pressure.

Treat five real minutes of progress as more valuable than another fifteen minutes of revisiting. If the conversation keeps reopening without closing, deliberately shrink its scope rather than hoping the next attempt will finally cover everything. Agree in advance to discuss exactly one narrow piece — just the power-of-attorney question, not the entire care plan — and treat fully resolving that one piece as complete success, even though larger questions remain. A series of small, actually-finished decisions outperforms a series of large, perpetually-open ones.

Track the conversation's history explicitly, in writing, so its repetition becomes impossible to ignore. A brief, shared note — even just a running list of dates the topic came up and what, if anything, got decided — makes the Zeigarnik-effect pattern visible in a way memory alone doesn't. Seeing "raised again, no resolution" recorded six or eight times tends to land with more force than simply sensing, vaguely, that this keeps happening, and that added force is often exactly what finally tips the next conversation from another rehearsal into an actual resolution.

The Rule to Remember: A conversation that keeps reopening isn't progress — it's the same door, opened and closed the same amount, every single time, until someone

decides to actually walk through it.

Chapter 7 — The Coverage You Know Is Wrong

Why Wanting the Perfect Choice Guarantees No Choice at All

He's read more about this specific topic than almost anyone he knows, which is precisely the problem. Three years ago, shortly after starting his own consulting practice, he began the process of finding better health and disability coverage than the bare-minimum policy he'd been carrying since leaving his last salaried job — a genuine, worthwhile goal, and one he approached with real diligence, comparing plans, reading independent reviews, consulting a broker, building his own comparison spreadsheet with more columns than the woman's rollover spreadsheet from Chapter 1. He knows, with real confidence, that his current coverage is inadequate for his actual situation — too high a deductible for his current income, gaps in the disability provisions that a self-employed person specifically should be covering, terms that made sense for the employee he used to be and don't fit the business owner he's become. He has known this for three years. He is still on the same inadequate policy.

What's kept him there isn't ignorance, and it isn't a failure to find reasonable alternatives — he's identified, at this point, no fewer than five different plans he considers genuinely solid, meaningfully better than his current one, any of which would represent real improvement if he simply picked one and switched. What's kept him frozen is a specific, persistent conviction that somewhere among those five, or perhaps among options he hasn't found yet, sits the actually correct answer — not a good answer, the correct one, the plan that optimally balances his specific risk profile, his specific cash flow, his specific long-term trajectory, in a way none of the five he's already found quite achieves. Every time he gets close to choosing one, a new consideration surfaces — a colleague mentions a provider network detail he hadn't weighted properly, an article raises a tax consideration specific to self-employed disability coverage he hadn't fully accounted for — and the search reopens, not because the current frontrunner has been disqualified, but because the possibility of something slightly better hasn't yet been fully ruled out.

A second scene shows a version of this same pattern applied to a much smaller, in principle simpler decision. A woman deciding how to structure college savings for her newborn daughter has spent months comparing account types, weighing tax advantages against flexibility, reading forum threads where parents debate the fine points of different approaches with a specificity that would be admirable if any of it were actually moving her closer to opening an account rather than further from it. She isn't confused about the broad strokes — any of the several reasonable, commonly recommended approaches would serve her daughter well, and she knows this, has been told this directly by more than one person she trusts. What she can't seem to do is accept "well-served" as sufficient when "optimally served" feels, somewhere just out of reach, like it should be achievable if she just does a little more comparison. Eighteen months into her daughter's life, the account still doesn't exist, and the tax-advantaged growth those eighteen months could have been generating is gone permanently, a cost that exists specifically because she was searching for the best possible account rather than accepting a genuinely good one.

A third scene involves a man selecting among several reasonable options for consolidating a handful of scattered accounts from an earlier career spent moving between jobs — old 401ks, a couple of small brokerage accounts, all candidates for a single, simpler structure. He's narrowed the field, competently, to three legitimate options, each recommended by different sources he trusts for different, defensible reasons. He describes his current state, when asked directly, as "just needing to pick one," a phrase that implies the decision is nearly finished, when in fact it's been in exactly this "just needing to pick one" state for over a year, because picking, for him, has come to feel like it requires a level of certainty that none of the three options, examined honestly, is ever going to provide — a certainty that, if he's honest with himself, no financial decision involving genuine uncertainty about the future could ever actually supply, regardless of how much additional comparison he does.

A fourth scene shows the pattern at its most consequential, involving a couple in their late fifties deciding how to structure a substantial portion of their retirement income once they stop working — an annuity, a systematic withdrawal plan, some blend of the two, each option carrying real, well-documented tradeoffs that no combination of further reading is going to fully resolve, because the actual best choice depends on how long each of them will live, information nobody can access in advance. They've met with two separate advisors, read a stack of books, built their own comparison spreadsheet not unlike the one from Chapter 1, and remain, eighteen months from their planned retirement date, exactly as undecided as they were when they started, not because either advisor gave them bad information, but because the decision itself contains an irreducible core of genuine uncertainty that no amount of additional research was ever going to eliminate — a fact that took them considerably longer to accept than it took them to gather the research in the first place.

What's actually happening

The distinction introduced in Chapter 2 between maximizing and satisficing, drawn from Herbert Simon's original 1956 research on bounded rationality and developed further by Barry Schwartz and his colleagues, applies here with even sharper force, because this chapter's pattern represents maximizing behavior operating at its most extreme and most self-defeating: not merely slowing a decision down, but preventing it from ever concluding at all. Simon's foundational insight — that a fully rational actor operating under genuine real-world constraints of time, information, and cognitive capacity should aim for a decision that clears a reasonable, well-defined threshold, rather than searching exhaustively for a theoretical optimum that may not even exist in any discoverable form — is worth restating precisely here, because the man comparing insurance plans has, in a real sense, inverted Simon's own definition of rationality. He believes, implicitly, that continuing to search represents the more careful, more responsible approach. Simon's research suggests the opposite: past a certain point, continued searching in the presence of several already-adequate options isn't more rational. It's a specific, well-documented failure mode of decision-making under uncertainty, mistaking exhaustiveness for diligence.

Schwartz's later research, extending the maximizing-satisficing distinction into real-world outcome measures, found something specifically relevant here: maximizers, across a range of studied decisions, don't actually end up with meaningfully better outcomes than satisficers in most cases — the fifth solid insurance plan and the first solid one tend to perform similarly well in practice, since all five cleared a genuine adequacy bar before being included in the comparison at all. What maximizers reliably do get, according to Schwartz's findings, is more decision-related distress, more time spent in the search process itself, and, in cases severe enough, no outcome at all, because the searching itself becomes the terminal state rather than a step toward one. This maps precisely onto all three scenes in this chapter: the consultant's five genuinely solid options, the mother's several genuinely reasonable account types, the man's three legitimate consolidation choices. None of these people are missing a good option. All of them are missing the willingness to stop looking for a better one once a good one has already, demonstrably, been found.

There's a further piece of research worth adding, from psychologist William Hick and, independently, Ray Hyman, whose separate studies in the early 1950s established what's since been called Hick's Law: a well-replicated finding that the time required to make a decision increases, in a measurable and fairly consistent way, as the number of available options increases — not linearly, but in a way that compounds as choices multiply and as the differences between those choices grow more subtle. Hick and Hyman's original research was conducted using simple, non-financial reaction-time tasks, but the underlying principle — that cognitive load and decision latency scale directly with option complexity — has since been repeatedly validated in more consequential, real-world decision contexts as well. This matters specifically for the man comparing consolidation options: his three choices aren't wildly different from each other on their face, which sounds like it should make the decision easier. Hick's Law suggests the opposite in exactly this case — when options are close in apparent quality, the fine-grained comparisons required to distinguish meaningfully between them actually take longer and feel less conclusive than when options are more obviously different, because there's no clear, dominant choice to anchor the decision quickly. Three closely matched good options can produce more decision paralysis than one obviously best option and two obviously worse ones would.

It's worth naming a further distinction that separates this chapter's pattern from earlier ones in the book, because the mechanism, while related to Chapter 2's choice overload, operates on a subtly different axis. Chapter 2 covered a decision frozen by the sheer number of options on the table. This chapter covers a decision frozen even after the options have already been thoughtfully, competently narrowed down to a genuinely manageable, high-quality shortlist — the freeze isn't coming from too many choices anymore. It's coming from an internal standard, self-imposed, that no finite amount of comparison among already-good options will ever fully satisfy, because the standard itself, "the objectively correct choice," isn't actually a coherent target in a domain — insurance, savings vehicles, account consolidation — where genuine future uncertainty means no amount of present-day analysis can ever produce full certainty about which option will, in hindsight, turn out to have been best.

There's a further piece of Schwartz's research worth adding, because it identifies a specific personality-level pattern behind who tends to fall into this trap most reliably. His follow-up studies found that maximizing tendency correlates significantly with perfectionism, and specifically with a subtype of perfectionism focused on avoiding mistakes rather than achieving a positive standard — a fear-based orientation rather than an aspiration-based one. This distinction matters for how the freeze actually feels from the inside: the consultant isn't searching because he's excited about finding something better. He's searching because stopping would mean accepting the possibility that a better option existed and he didn't find it, a possibility that a mistake-avoidant perfectionist finds specifically, disproportionately uncomfortable, compared to someone motivated by simply wanting a good outcome. The search, understood this way, isn't really about the insurance at all. It's about never having to be the person who settled for good enough when perfect might have been out there.

What it costs you

The most direct cost in every scene in this chapter is identical in shape: the inadequate current arrangement — under-covered, unopened, unconsolidated — continues operating exactly as it currently does for every additional month the maximizing search continues, and in every case, the actual, real-world difference between the eventual choice and any of the already-identified good alternatives is almost certainly smaller than the cost of the additional delay itself. The consultant's inadequate disability coverage remains inadequate for a fourth year running, exposing him to real risk the entire time, in service of a search unlikely to produce meaningfully better terms than the five options already sitting on his desk. The mother's daughter loses eighteen months, and counting, of tax-advantaged growth that no eventual account choice, however optimal, can ever retroactively recover.

There's a second cost specific to this pattern worth naming: Schwartz's research on maximizers found a further, somewhat counterintuitive result — maximizers who do eventually make a decision tend to report lower satisfaction with the outcome than satisficers report with their own, objectively comparable choices, because the exhaustive search process trains a heightened awareness of everything the chosen option lacks relative to whatever else might theoretically exist. The irony compounds: the search that was meant to produce the most satisfying possible outcome tends to produce a less satisfying experience of whatever outcome is eventually reached, on top of the extended cost of the delay itself.

A third cost follows from Hick's Law specifically: continued searching among closely matched options doesn't just fail to produce a clearer answer — it can actively erode the decision-maker's confidence in their own judgment over time, since repeated cycles of "these all seem similarly good, but I still don't feel sure" teach the searcher, gradually, that their own assessment can't be trusted to conclude anything, a lesson that then generalizes to future decisions well beyond the one currently stuck.

A fourth cost ties to the mistake-avoidant perfectionism described above: because the underlying fear is about being wrong rather than about achieving a specific outcome, the search rarely stays contained to a single decision. The same mistake-avoidant orientation that keeps the consultant comparing insurance plans tends to show up again the next time he faces a comparable decision — a new savings vehicle, a new advisor, a new major purchase — meaning the true cost of this pattern isn't measured in one delayed decision, but in a recurring tax on every future decision that shares the same basic shape, each one liable to trigger the identical search-without-end unless the underlying orientation itself gets named and addressed directly.

A fifth cost is specific to the retirement-income scene: unlike a rollover or a rebalance, some of the decisions this chapter covers involve options that don't stay equally available forever. Certain annuity products, certain enrollment windows, certain rate locks are priced against conditions that shift over time — meaning a couple who spend eighteen months maximizing their way toward the theoretically perfect retirement-income structure may find, when they finally do decide, that some of the specific options they were comparing eighteen months earlier no longer exist on the same terms. The search for the perfect answer, in these specific cases, doesn't just delay a good outcome. It can quietly narrow the field of good outcomes still available by the time the search finally, reluctantly, concludes.

One clarification before the overrides, because it matters for how you'll use them: none of what follows is an argument against careful comparison in general. Comparing thoughtfully before committing to a five-figure insurance decision or a college savings vehicle is genuinely responsible. The line this chapter draws is narrower and more specific — between comparison that's still adding real information and comparison that's continuing purely because stopping feels like it requires more certainty than the situation will ever actually provide.

The overrides

Set an explicit, numeric "good enough" threshold before comparing any specific options. Before evaluating any actual plans, accounts, or alternatives, write down the specific criteria a choice needs to meet to be acceptable — not optimal, acceptable — and commit, in writing, that the first option meeting every criterion on that list is the one you'll select. This directly counters the internal, undefined "objectively correct" standard driving the freeze, replacing it with a concrete, satisfiable target that actually can be met, rather than an abstract standard that, by its nature, never quite can be.

The Move: eliminate the two weakest of your shortlisted options entirely, permanently, right now. If you've already narrowed a decision to three or more genuinely solid choices, as all three people in this chapter had, don't keep them all in play "just in case." Actively discard all but two, based on whatever criteria matter most to you, and commit that you will choose between only those two, this week. Hick's Law suggests that shrinking a close field from three or more down to two dramatically reduces decision latency, even when the discarded options were perfectly reasonable — the goal isn't finding the theoretical best among many. It's making a good decision from a genuinely small, final field.

Set a fixed, non-negotiable decision date and treat it as a deadline with real consequences, not a soft target. Borrowing directly from Chapter 6's override: an open-ended search, per Steel's temporal motivation research, will expand to fill whatever time is available to it, because there's no natural stopping point built into the search itself. Manufacture that stopping point deliberately — two weeks from today, say — and commit, in advance, that if no clear winner has emerged by that date, you will select whichever remaining option is highest-ranked at that moment, no further deliberation permitted.

Ask what a satisficer, not a maximizer, would have already done. When you notice yourself reopening a search that's already produced multiple adequate answers, pause and ask directly: if I simply needed this to be good rather than perfect, would I already have chosen? For nearly every decision in this chapter's territory, the honest answer is yes — which reveals that the ongoing search isn't actually about finding a better answer anymore. It's about avoiding the discomfort of closing the search at all.

Remind yourself, explicitly, that future information will always exist, and waiting for it doesn't actually reduce genuine uncertainty about the future. Part of what fuels the endless search is an implicit belief that just a little more research will finally produce real certainty. It won't, because the actual source of uncertainty — how the future unfolds — isn't something more comparison-shopping among present-day options can resolve. Accepting this directly, rather than continuing to search as though certainty were one more article away, is often the single most useful mental step available.

Ask a satisficer you trust to make the final call for you, if the maximizing pull is especially strong. Sometimes the fastest way out of a mistake-avoidant search isn't a personal technique at all — it's deliberately handing the final selection to someone else, a partner, a friend, an advisor, who doesn't carry the same fear of being wrong. Give them the shortlist and the criteria, and let their outside, less personally invested judgment supply the closing decision your own perfectionism keeps refusing to supply on its own.

The Rule to Remember: You were never actually choosing between five good options — you were choosing between having decent coverage starting today and having no coverage at all while you kept looking for perfect.

Chapter 8 — The Raise That Never Reached Your Savings Rate

Why a Change That Costs Nothing Still Doesn't Happen

The raise landed eight months ago, a genuinely meaningful increase, the kind that comes with an actual title change and a real sense that something has shifted in her career. She remembers the specific feeling of seeing the new number on her first updated pay stub, a small private thrill that she's since described to a friend as "one of those moments where you think, okay, now I'll finally get serious about saving more." She had, at the time, a specific and entirely reasonable plan: increase her retirement contribution percentage to match the raise, so that the additional income would flow directly into savings before she had a chance to adjust her lifestyle around it, before the raise became simply the new normal amount of money she has, indistinguishable from what came before. It was, by her own account, an obviously good plan, costing her nothing in any meaningful sense — she wasn't going to miss money she'd never had before, spent according to a budget she'd never gotten used to. Eight months later, the contribution percentage sits exactly where it sat before the raise. The additional income has, in fact, become simply the new normal amount of money she has — precisely the outcome the plan was designed to prevent, achieved entirely on its own, without her doing anything to stop it.

What's notable about this particular freeze, compared to several others in this book, is how genuinely low the stakes of actually acting would have been. Increasing a contribution percentage on an existing account, through a portal she's used before, for a change that would cost her nothing she's currently used to spending, is about as close to a frictionless financial decision as exists — closer, certainly, than rolling over an old account, closer than drafting a will, closer than navigating a difficult shared conversation. And yet eight months have passed with the change unmade, not through any specific obstacle, but through the same quiet, accumulating deferral this entire book has been describing: an intention formed once, at a moment of genuine motivation, that never quite converted into the three-minute action it would have taken to lock in, before the motivation itself faded into the background the way motivation reliably does once the initial excitement of a raise settles into the ordinary rhythm of a normal paycheck.

A second scene shows a related version of this freeze playing out over a slightly longer arc. A man who paid off a car loan eighteen months ago had, at the time, a clear and specific intention to redirect the monthly payment amount — a real, meaningful sum he was already comfortably living without, since it had been leaving his account automatically every month for years — directly into an investment account, on the theory that since he'd never miss the money in his day-to-day budget, converting the freed-up payment into savings would be, in his own words at the time, "basically free money I'm just choosing to keep giving to myself instead of the bank." He set up the automatic transfer within a week of the final loan payment, genuinely following through on the initial intention. What he didn't anticipate was how quickly the freed-up amount, sitting visibly larger in his checking account each month before the transfer executed a few days later, would start feeling available for other things — a slightly nicer dinner out here, a slightly less careful month there — until, four months in, he quietly reduced the automatic transfer amount "just for this month," and then again the following month, until the transfer that was meant to capture the full freed-up payment now captures less than half of it, with the remainder simply absorbed into an ordinary spending pattern that expanded, almost invisibly, to fill the space the loan payment used to occupy.

A third scene involves a couple who received a modest but real windfall — a small inheritance, invested conservatively per the deceased relative's own long-standing wishes, generating a small but genuine amount of passive income each year that neither of them had budgeted for or planned around, since it simply began appearing as a matter of course once the inheritance was invested. They agreed, in the first year, that this income should be redirected entirely toward an underfunded emergency fund they both knew needed rebuilding after a difficult stretch a few years earlier. For the first several months, it was: the income arrived, and they moved it, deliberately, into the emergency fund, exactly as planned. Somewhere around month six, without either of them making an explicit decision to change course, a portion of that income started simply staying in the checking account it arrived in, covering an unplanned expense here, absorbed into an unusually expensive month there, until, by the two-year mark, the redirection had quietly stopped happening altogether, and neither of them could point to the specific month it had stopped, only that it clearly had.

A fourth scene involves a self-employed consultant who successfully negotiated a meaningfully higher rate with her largest client at the start of the year, and who had, at the time, resolved to keep her own monthly draw from the business exactly where it had been, directing the entire increase toward her own retirement contributions, since her old rate had already been supporting her comfortably. For the first quarter, the plan held. By the second quarter, a handful of one-off business expenses — a new laptop, a conference she decided was worth attending — got quietly paid out of the increased revenue rather than treated as expenses to plan around separately, and by year's end, reviewing her numbers with her accountant, she discovered that the meaningfully higher rate had produced a barely noticeable increase in what she'd actually redirected toward retirement, the rest having been absorbed, one reasonable-sounding exception at a time, into a slightly more comfortable version of exactly the same business operations as before.

What's actually happening

The psychologists Thomas Gilovich and Victoria Medvec, in a 1994 paper examining the temporal pattern of regret, uncovered a finding that helps explain why decisions like this one — genuinely costless, genuinely beneficial, genuinely easy to execute — still so reliably fail to get locked in and sustained. Their research distinguished between regret over actions and regret over inactions, and found something the researchers themselves described as counterintuitive at the time: in the short term, immediately following a decision, people report more regret over actions taken than over actions not taken — a bad outcome resulting from something you actively did stings more, in the moment, than a bad outcome resulting from something you simply didn't do. But Gilovich and Medvec found this pattern reversed over longer time horizons: asked to reflect on regrets from years or decades earlier, people consistently reported more regret over inactions — the things they didn't do, didn't pursue, didn't lock in — than over actions they'd taken and had go poorly.

This asymmetry maps directly onto the raise scenario, in a way worth spelling out precisely. In the immediate aftermath of the raise, locking in a higher contribution percentage feels, faintly, like an action with a downside worth weighing — a small, immediate reduction in take-home pay, a small, immediate adjustment to a lifestyle that could, in principle, have simply absorbed the entire raise instead. That immediate, action-framed downside, however small, registers more vividly in the moment than the much larger, but distant and abstract, inaction-framed cost of never having locked the increase in at all — a cost that, per Gilovich and Medvec's research, would only fully register as genuine regret years later, once the compounding gap between "what I would have saved" and "what I actually saved" has become large enough to notice and mourn. The short-term calculation favors staying with the familiar spending pattern. The long-term calculation, which almost nobody actually runs in the moment a raise lands, would favor locking the increase in immediately. Gilovich and

Medvec's research explains precisely why the short-term calculation wins so reliably: it's the one the mind is actually weighing in real time, while the long-term one sits dormant until it's too late to matter.

There's a further mechanism at work in the car-loan and inheritance scenes specifically, worth naming directly: both involve a freed-up or newly arriving sum of money gradually, almost invisibly, absorbing itself into ordinary spending through a process that doesn't require any single deliberate decision to reverse the original intention — it happens through a long series of small, individually reasonable-seeming exceptions, each one easy to justify on its own terms, that collectively undo a commitment nobody ever consciously chose to abandon. This connects to a broader finding in behavioral economics about what's sometimes called "mental accounting drift" — a concept building on Richard Thaler's foundational work on mental accounting, which established that people don't treat money as perfectly fungible, instead assigning it to specific mental categories that shape how freely it gets spent. Money newly arriving without an established, defended category — a freed-up loan payment with no firm label yet, a windfall's income stream not yet fully locked into a specific purpose — is considerably more vulnerable to gradual reclassification into general, unrestricted spending than money that's been assigned a firm, defended category from the very start. The couple's redirection succeeded for six months precisely because the income had a clear, defended label — "emergency fund money" — and began failing the moment small exceptions started chipping away at that label's firmness, one reasonable-sounding override at a time.

It's worth naming why this chapter's pattern, despite involving genuinely low-friction, low-cost decisions, still belongs squarely in this book rather than reading as a simple lack of discipline. The freeze here isn't about difficulty executing a single action — the initial step, in every scene, actually did get taken (the woman knew what to do, the man set up the transfer, the couple started the redirection). The freeze is about *sustaining* a decision against the slow, cumulative pull of Gilovich and Medvec's short-term regret asymmetry and Thaler's mental-accounting drift, both of which erode a good decision gradually, invisibly, through no single moment anyone would recognize as "the moment I decided to stop." That's precisely the shape of paralysis this book is built around: not a dramatic single failure to act, but a quiet, cumulative failure to keep acting, indistinguishable, from the inside, from never having decided anything at all.

There's a further piece of research worth adding here, from the psychologist Philip Brickman and colleagues' foundational work on hedonic adaptation — the well-documented finding that people adjust remarkably quickly to changes in their circumstances, including financial ones, with a new income level or a new baseline of available spending money settling into "normal" far faster than most people expect. This matters directly for understanding why the raise stops feeling like extra money within weeks rather than staying, indefinitely, in some mental category of "bonus income I haven't gotten used to yet." Hedonic adaptation research suggests there's a genuinely narrow window — measured in weeks, not months — during which a new sum of money still feels psychologically distinct from a person's established baseline, and once that window closes, the money has functionally merged into the ordinary paycheck, no longer available to be redirected without triggering the same felt sense of active loss that redirecting any other ordinary income would trigger. The plan formed the week of the raise wasn't just a good idea that faded from memory. It was racing against a closing biological window the whole time, whether the woman in this chapter's opening scene realized it or not.

What it costs you

The direct cost compounds specifically because this is the single easiest, lowest-effort action to get right in this entire book, and the compounding effect of losing it is proportionally larger than almost anything else covered so far: money that would have been captured automatically, at zero ongoing effort, from month one of a raise or a freed-up payment, instead never enters the compounding pool at all, and every month of delay isn't recoverable later at the same value — a dollar not saved in the first year after a raise doesn't just represent that one dollar; it represents that dollar's entire subsequent growth trajectory, permanently forfeited, in a way no later increase in savings rate can retroactively restore.

It's worth making this concrete rather than leaving it abstract, because vague awareness of compounding rarely moves anyone the way a specific comparison does. A person who locks in an increase the week a raise arrives and a person who locks in the identical increase five years later, at the identical dollar amount, do not end up in the same place, even though both eventually "did the right thing." The first person's money has had five additional years to grow before the second person's even started; depending on the size of the raise and the years remaining until retirement, that head start alone can represent a genuinely substantial share of the account's eventual value — not because the five-years-late saver did anything wrong once they finally acted, but because the specific years right after a raise, when the money is easiest to redirect without any felt sacrifice, are also, mechanically, the years where each dollar redirected has the most time left to compound. The window that closes quietly in this chapter isn't just an opportunity. It's the single highest-value window in this entire book, precisely because it costs nothing and compounds the longest.

There's a second cost specific to the gradual, undetected nature of this pattern: because the erosion happens through a long series of small, individually reasonable exceptions rather than one identifiable bad decision, it's considerably harder to catch and correct than a single frozen task sitting visibly undone in a drawer. The man with the car loan doesn't experience a moment of realizing he's stopped saving the full freed-up payment — by the time anyone checks the actual numbers against the original plan, months or years may have passed, and the gap between intention and reality has grown large enough to represent a genuinely significant sum, discovered all at once rather than caught early when the correction would have been smaller and easier.

A third cost follows from Gilovich and Medvec's longer-horizon finding specifically: because inaction regret arrives late, often years after the relevant window has closed, the people in these scenes are unlikely to feel the full weight of what's been lost until it's no longer correctable — the raise from eight months ago cannot be "re-captured" retroactively at its original compounding value, no matter how motivated a future version of the person becomes. The cost isn't just financial. It's the specific, delayed, and ultimately unavoidable regret that Gilovich and Medvec's research identifies as the dominant long-term pattern — a regret this book's readers are, in a real sense, being warned about in advance, with enough lead time to actually do something different.

A fourth cost ties to the closing-window dynamic described above: because hedonic adaptation happens quickly and largely outside conscious awareness, each missed window doesn't just cost the specific raise or windfall involved — it trains a repeating pattern across an entire career. Most people receive several raises, several freed-up payments, several unplanned sums of money over a working lifetime, and a person who's missed the window once, without understanding why, is likely to miss it again at the next opportunity, and the one after that, each time experiencing the same brief flicker of good intention followed by the same quiet, untraceable absorption into ordinary spending — a pattern that, left unexamined, can repeat itself a dozen times across a career without ever once being recognized as the same recurring event.

The overrides

Lock the increase in at the source, before the money ever reaches a spendable account. The single most effective override for this chapter's specific pattern is structural rather than psychological: increase a retirement contribution percentage, or redirect a freed-up payment, through an automatic, payroll-level or bank-level mechanism that moves the money before it ever lands somewhere it could be spent, rather than relying on willpower to redirect money that's already sitting, visible and available, in a checking account. This directly targets the mental-accounting drift mechanism — money that never gets a chance to be reclassified as "just what I have now" can't gradually erode the way money sitting in an undefended general account can.

The Move: act within 72 hours of the triggering event, before the new baseline sets in. Gilovich and Medvec's research on regret is compounded by a related, well-established finding on how quickly people adapt to a new financial baseline

— the longer a raise, a freed-up payment, or a windfall sits unallocated in ordinary spending, the more thoroughly it gets absorbed into the new "normal," and the harder it becomes to redirect without it feeling like an active cut rather than simply not spending money you never really had. Make the increase, the redirection, or the reallocation within three days of the triggering event — before the higher paycheck, the freed-up payment, or the windfall has had a chance to become the new normal in your own mind.

Give the redirected money a firm, specific, named label from day one — and defend the label explicitly when the first exception tempts you. Following Thaler's mental accounting research directly: money with a clear, specific purpose attached ("the freed-up car payment, going to my investment account, no exceptions") resists reclassification far more effectively than money simply sitting, unlabeled, in a general account. The first time you're tempted to make a "just this once" exception, recognize it explicitly for what it is — the first crack in the label, not a harmless one-time adjustment — because Thaler's research and this chapter's scenes both show that the first exception rarely stays the only one.

Set a recurring check, on a fixed schedule, that compares the current reality against the original plan. Because this chapter's erosion happens gradually and often invisibly, catching it requires a deliberate, scheduled comparison rather than hoping it will be noticed naturally. Every six months, compare the actual contribution percentage, transfer amount, or redirection against the original commitment, in writing, and treat any gap as something to close immediately rather than something to note and revisit later.

Reframe the decision using the long-horizon regret Gilovich and Medvec's research actually found, not the short-horizon one your mind defaults to. Before deciding whether to keep, reduce, or skip a planned increase, deliberately ask the long-horizon question rather than the short-horizon one: not "will I miss this money this month," but "in twenty years, which will I regret more — the modest adjustment I made this month, or the money I never let myself save because it never felt urgent enough to lock in." Gilovich and Medvec's own research suggests you already know the honest answer to that question.

The trick is asking it before the moment passes, not years later when it's the only question left.

Track every raise, freed-up payment, and windfall on a single running list, so the pattern becomes visible across your whole career rather than invisible within any single instance. Because hedonic adaptation makes each individual missed window nearly impossible to notice in the moment, keep one running record — the date, the amount, whether it was captured or absorbed — so that a repeated pattern, if it exists, shows up clearly the next time you review it, rather than staying hidden inside a series of individually forgettable Tuesdays.

The Rule to Remember: The easiest money you'll ever save is the money you never let yourself get used to having — and the only window to save it is the one that's closing right now, while it still feels new.

Chapter 9 — The Statement You Skim But Never Act On

Why Too Many Right Answers Feel Like No Answer

The quarterly statement arrives, as it has for years, and he reads it — actually reads it, cover to cover, in a way that would surprise anyone who assumed, reasonably enough given everything else this book has described, that the pattern here would involve avoidance. It doesn't. He's not the kind of person this book's sister volume on shame would recognize; there's no flinch, no dread, no unopened envelope. He reads the performance summary, the fee disclosures, the fund-by-fund breakdown, genuinely engaged with all of it, often making small mental notes about things worth revisiting — a fund that's underperformed its category for three straight quarters, a fee that seems slightly higher than what he recalls from a comparable option elsewhere, an allocation percentage that no longer quite matches what he'd choose if he were building the portfolio fresh today. He finishes reading, sets the statement in a specific pile on his desk reserved for exactly this purpose, and goes back to his day, having genuinely absorbed everything in it and genuinely acted on none of it — not this quarter, not the quarter before, not, if he's honest, in longer than he'd like to admit when he actually stops to count.

What makes this scene distinct from most of the others in this book is that he isn't missing information, and he isn't frozen by a single hard decision he's avoiding. He's frozen by the sheer number of individually small, individually reasonable actions the statement surfaces every single quarter, none of which feels urgent enough, on its own, to justify interrupting his day to address immediately, and all of which, together, add up to a genuinely substantial list he's never once, across years of quarterly statements, sat down and worked through systematically. The underperforming fund could be switched. The fee could be questioned or moved elsewhere. The allocation could be adjusted. Any one of these, examined alone, is a fifteen-minute task. All of them together, appearing quarter after quarter, form a backlog that's grown large enough that even beginning to address it now feels like it requires setting aside an entire afternoon he never quite finds — not because the individual tasks are hard, but because there are enough of them, sitting in enough different categories, that picking where to actually start has itself become a kind of decision he keeps deferring.

A second scene shows the same pattern at a smaller, earlier scale, useful because it demonstrates the freeze doesn't require years of accumulated backlog to take hold. A woman two years into actively managing her own investment accounts for the first time reads a monthly summary email from her brokerage that flags, routinely and automatically, three or four specific "opportunities" each month — a tax-loss harvesting suggestion, a fund with a lower expense ratio in the same category as one she holds, a note that her cash allocation has drifted above her stated target. She reads every one of these emails closely, genuinely interested, and has, in two years, acted on almost none of them, not because any single suggestion seems wrong, but because by the time she's finished reading the third one, the first one no longer feels as urgent as it did a few minutes earlier, and by the time she's back at her desk the following week, the entire email has faded into the general, undifferentiated backdrop of "things I should look into," a category so large by this point that nothing in it ever quite rises to the top.

A third scene involves a small nonprofit's part-time treasurer, a volunteer role handled by someone with real financial competence in her actual career, who receives detailed monthly reports on the organization's modest investment reserve — reports that reliably surface two or three small, easily-actionable items each month: a signature still needed on an updated document, a small reallocation the organization's own investment policy calls for given a recent market move, a minor administrative update to a contact or beneficiary on file. She reads every report thoroughly, understands every item completely, and has developed, over her three years in the role, a quiet, private sense of embarrassment about how large the list of small unaddressed items has grown, a list she now avoids mentioning directly to the board not because she's hiding anything consequential, but because naming the full list out loud, all at once, would make its size suddenly, uncomfortably visible in a way that reading each individual monthly report, one small item at a time, has never quite forced her to confront.

A fourth scene shows the identical pattern operating over a much shorter time horizon, useful because it demonstrates the mechanism doesn't require years to take hold. A man newly enrolled in his first employer-sponsored health savings account receives, over his first ninety days, a series of onboarding emails from the plan administrator, each one flagging a specific, simple optional action — electing a preferred investment mix for the account balance above a certain threshold, naming a beneficiary, opting into a slightly higher contribution rate that would maximize the employer match. Each email, read individually, describes an easy five-minute task with an obvious right answer. By the sixth email, arriving in his seventh week, he no longer opens them promptly, not from any decision to ignore the account, but because the accumulating, undifferentiated sense of "several things I still need to do here" has already begun to feel heavier than any single item actually warrants — a compressed, ninety-day version of the multi-year backlog the treasurer and the statement-reader are each managing on a longer clock.

What's actually happening

The Hick's Law research introduced in Chapter 7 — the finding, from William Hick and Ray Hyman's independent work in the early 1950s, that decision time increases measurably as the number of available options grows — applies here in a distinct and important variation worth naming directly. Chapter 7 covered a single decision frozen by too many competing options at one moment in time. This chapter's pattern is different: it's not one decision with many options, but many small, individually simple decisions, each with a clear right answer, arriving faster than any one of them gets fully resolved before the next one arrives. The cognitive burden isn't in comparing alternatives within a single choice — each item on the statement or in the monthly email is, considered alone, a straightforward action with an obvious answer. The burden is in triage: deciding which of several equally legitimate, equally small tasks to address first, a decision that, per the broader principle Hick and Hyman's research points toward, itself takes measurably longer and feels measurably less conclusive as the list of competing small tasks grows, even though every individual item on that list would be trivial to resolve in isolation.

There's a related and important concept worth introducing here, drawn from research on what's sometimes called decision fatigue — a broad body of findings, developed across multiple researchers studying willpower and self-regulation, suggesting that the capacity to make deliberate, effortful decisions is a finite resource that depletes with use over the course of a day, making later decisions more likely to default to the path of least resistance regardless of that decision's actual merit. Applied to the statement-reading scene: by the time a reader has processed an entire quarterly statement's worth of performance data, fee disclosures, and allocation details — a genuinely effortful cognitive task in its own right — the specific, separate decisions that statement surfaces (switch this fund, question this fee, rebalance this allocation) are being evaluated by a mind that's already spent a meaningful amount of its available decision-making capacity simply reading and comprehending the document that raised them. The reading itself, ironically, uses up some of the very capacity that would be needed to act on what's been read.

There's a further piece of the mechanism worth naming, connecting back to the Zeigarnik effect introduced in Chapter 6: each unaddressed small item from a previous statement doesn't fully disappear once a new statement arrives — it remains, per Zeigarnik's original research on unfinished tasks, a low-grade open loop, and a growing collection of these open loops, accumulating quarter after quarter or month after month, creates a compounding cognitive burden that makes engaging with any new statement progressively heavier over time, even though the specific new items it raises are, individually, exactly as simple as the very first item ever flagged, years earlier, when the whole pattern started. The treasurer's quiet embarrassment about the size of her accumulated list is a direct, felt experience of this compounding: the individual items were never hard. Their accumulated number is what's become genuinely heavy to face.

It's worth distinguishing this chapter's pattern precisely from Chapter 3's omission bias, because the two can look similar from a distance but operate through different mechanisms. Chapter 3 covered a single, specific form frozen by a fear of getting it wrong. This chapter's pattern involves no comparable fear — none of these three people report any anxiety about correctly switching a fund or questioning a fee; they're confident in their ability to execute any single item correctly. What's freezing them isn't fear of error. It's the combined weight of triage difficulty (Hick's Law, applied to competing small tasks rather than competing large options), depleted decision-making capacity by the time each item is actually considered (decision fatigue), and a growing backlog of unresolved open loops compounding the felt weight of every new item that arrives (the Zeigarnik effect, operating cumulatively rather than on a single task). Three genuinely distinct mechanisms, working together, producing a freeze that looks, from the outside, like simple procrastination, but that responds to a different set of interventions than procrastination alone would.

There's a further piece of research worth adding here, from psychologist Barry Schwartz's broader writing on choice architecture, which distinguishes between decisions that arrive as a single bounded event and decisions that arrive as an ongoing, recurring stream — a distinction with real consequences for which overrides actually work. A single frozen decision, once resolved, stays resolved; there's a clear before-and-after. A recurring stream of small decisions, by contrast, never offers that same clean resolution, because resolving this quarter's list does nothing to prevent next quarter's from beginning to accumulate all over again unless the underlying system generating the stream is itself changed. This is precisely why the treasurer's situation feels so much heavier than a single overdue form: she isn't facing one backlog to clear. She's facing a backlog-generating process that will keep producing new items indefinitely, at the same pace, regardless of how thoroughly she works through the current one — which means, without a structural fix to the process itself, even a fully cleared backlog today guarantees nothing about the state of the list six months from now.

What it costs you

The direct financial cost compounds across every unaddressed item on every statement, in ways that mirror several earlier chapters but at a larger aggregate scale: the underperforming fund continues underperforming, the excess fee continues accruing, quarter after quarter, and because these items arrive continuously rather than as a single decision point, the total accumulated cost of the full backlog is frequently larger than any single chapter's individual pattern, simply because it represents years of small, compounding neglect across multiple simultaneous fronts rather than one frozen decision.

There's a second cost specific to this chapter's compounding-backlog structure: the size of the list itself becomes a genuine barrier to ever starting, in a way that a single frozen task doesn't produce. A person facing one unrolled 401k can, per Chapter 1's overrides, shrink the task to its smallest unit and begin. A person facing a three-year accumulation of small quarterly items faces something psychologically heavier — not one small task, but the prospect of an entire afternoon spent working through a long list, which itself starts to feel like a project requiring its own scheduling and preparation, exactly the kind of larger, more effortful undertaking this book has repeatedly shown gets deferred far more easily than a small one.

A third cost is specific to the treasurer's scene: an accumulated, unaddressed backlog that a responsible party is aware of but hasn't disclosed or acted on carries a distinct professional and reputational risk beyond the underlying financial cost — the longer it goes unaddressed, the harder it becomes to raise it without the raising itself appearing to be an admission of extended neglect, which creates a perverse incentive to keep the backlog quiet rather than surface it, deepening the very freeze that created it in the first place.

A fourth cost ties to the recurring-stream structure described above: without a fix to the underlying process, every override that only addresses the *current* backlog is, at best, a temporary reprieve. The woman reading her monthly summary emails could, in principle, spend an afternoon acting on two years of accumulated flagged items and feel a genuine, well-earned sense of relief — and then watch an identical backlog begin rebuilding the very next month, at the identical pace, because nothing about how she processes each new email has actually changed. The cost of treating a recurring pattern as a one-time cleanup, rather than recognizing it as an ongoing system requiring an ongoing fix, is a relief that never lasts as long as it should.

There's a fifth cost worth adding, specific to the newly enrolled man's ninety-day scene: a backlog that begins accumulating early, right at the start of a new financial relationship — a new employer's benefits, a first brokerage account, a first HSA — has an outsized effect on the habits that get built around that relationship going forward. The pattern set in the first ninety days tends to become the default pattern for the life of the account, which means an early backlog isn't just a delayed set of small tasks. It's the founding template for how every future item from that same source will be handled, for years, unless something interrupts it deliberately before the pattern has a chance to fully set.

One note before the overrides: because this chapter's pattern is a recurring stream rather than a single event, the fix has to be structural and durable, not a one-time cleanup effort. Each override below is built to change the ongoing process itself, so the backlog stops regenerating rather than simply getting cleared once and left to rebuild on its own schedule.

The overrides

Process each statement in real time, the moment you read it, rather than filing it for later. The single most effective structural change here is collapsing the gap between reading and acting to as close to zero as possible. When an item surfaces — a fund flagged, a fee noted, an allocation drifted — take the smallest possible action on it immediately, before moving to the next line of the statement, rather than mentally noting it and continuing to read. This prevents the Zeigarnik-effect backlog from ever accumulating in the first place, which is considerably easier than clearing an existing one.

The Move: if a backlog already exists, triage it into exactly three categories, once, and work only one category at a time. Facing an accumulated list, don't attempt to address everything at once — that's precisely the kind of large, effortful undertaking this book has shown gets deferred. Instead, sort the full list, in a single sitting, into three simple buckets: things costing real money right now (fees, underperformance), things with a real time-sensitivity (a signature, a deadline), and things that are correct but not urgent (a minor drift, an optional optimization). Address the first bucket completely before touching the second, and the second completely before touching the third. This converts an undifferentiated, overwhelming backlog into a small number of genuinely manageable, sequential tasks.

Set a hard cap on how many new items you'll evaluate per statement, and defer the rest deliberately, in writing, rather than by default. If a single statement or report reliably surfaces more actionable items than you can realistically address before decision fatigue sets in, choose the two or three most consequential ones per cycle, address those fully, and explicitly, in writing, note the remainder as intentionally deferred to the next cycle — a small distinction, but an important one, because deliberately deferred items don't accumulate the same open-loop weight that silently unaddressed ones do.

Separate the reading of the statement from the acting on it, on purpose, with a scheduled gap between the two. Because decision fatigue research suggests the act of reading and comprehending a dense financial document depletes some of the very capacity needed to act on what it reveals, read the statement once for comprehension, then close it, and return to it a day or two later, specifically to act, with fresh decision-making capacity available rather than capacity already spent on the reading itself.

Name the backlog out loud to someone else, deliberately, before it grows large enough that naming it feels like a confession. The treasurer's specific bind — a backlog too embarrassing to raise, growing larger because it's never raised — is best interrupted early, before shame attaches to the list's size. If you manage a shared or overseen account, mention any accumulating list to a co-owner, advisor, or oversight body while it's still small and unremarkable, establishing a precedent of routine disclosure before the list ever becomes large enough to feel like something requiring an explanation.

Redesign the source itself, if you have any control over it, to surface fewer, better-prioritized items rather than an undifferentiated stream. If a brokerage or reporting tool lets you adjust alert frequency or filter by significance, use that control deliberately — fewer, more clearly ranked items reduce the triage burden described in this chapter far more effectively than any personal discipline applied to an unfiltered stream ever will, because the fix happens upstream, before the decision fatigue and the Zeigarnik-effect backlog even have a chance to start accumulating.

The Rule to Remember: A right answer you read and don't act on isn't information anymore — it's just a longer list, and the list doesn't get easier to face by getting longer.

Chapter 10 — The Five Minutes That Breaks the Freeze

Why One Small, Pre-Committed Action Undoes Years of Deferral

Every scene in this book so far has ended the same way most real financial freezes actually end, when they end at all — not in a single, dramatic moment of resolve, but in something smaller and less cinematic than that. The woman with the old 401k eventually rolled it over, not on some triumphant morning of finally feeling ready, but on an ordinary Tuesday when she'd committed, in advance, to spending exactly the amount of time it took to find the account login, and then, having done that one small thing, found the next step meaningfully easier than the whole task had looked from a distance. The man with the beneficiary form finally signed it, not because his fear of making a mistake disappeared, but because he'd asked a friend to glance over the completed draft first, which shrank the actual risk down to something his fear could no longer inflate quite as effectively. Every override in every chapter of this book has pointed toward the same underlying move, dressed in different specific clothes each time: shrink the decision down to something small enough that the freeze, which defends effectively against large, ambiguous, emotionally loaded tasks, simply doesn't have enough surface area to grab onto.

This final chapter is about that move itself, examined directly, because it turns out to be the one mechanism running underneath every single override this book has offered — and understanding it explicitly, rather than only encountering it piecemeal chapter by chapter, makes it available for whatever frozen decision this book hasn't specifically covered, the ones unique to your own particular financial life that no chapter here happened to describe exactly.

Consider a scene that ties several of this book's earlier threads together. A woman in her forties, reading back over her own situation honestly after working through material very much like what this book has covered, identifies four separate frozen decisions in her own financial life at once — an old account never rolled over, a beneficiary form never updated, a will never finalized, a rebalance overdue by at least two years. Faced with the full list, laid out plainly, she feels something close to what the treasurer in Chapter 9 felt facing her own accumulated backlog: a kind of paralysis about the paralysis itself, an overwhelming sense that fixing four significant things at once is its own kind of impossible task, larger and more daunting than any single item on the list. What actually breaks this particular freeze — and it does break, over the following six weeks, all four items eventually resolved — isn't a burst of motivation or a newly discovered reserve of willpower. It's a specific, deliberately small first commitment: she decides, the evening she makes the list, to spend exactly five minutes, that same evening, on exactly one of the four items — not resolving it, just beginning it, in whatever small way beginning is possible in five minutes. She finds the phone number for the old plan provider. That's the entire five minutes. She writes it down, closes her laptop, and goes to bed.

The five minutes matter enormously, and it's worth being precise about why, because the actual content of what got done in them — finding a phone number — is trivially small, almost embarrassingly so relative to the size of the problem it's meant to address. What the five minutes accomplished wasn't progress on the task in any meaningful practical sense. It was proof, delivered directly to her own nervous system rather than merely to her intellect, that the task could be started without the catastrophe some unnamed part of her had apparently been quietly expecting. Nothing bad happened. No overwhelming wave of anxiety or confusion arrived. The five minutes simply ended, having been spent, having produced a small, real result. That proof, repeated the following evening with a second small five-minute commitment toward a different item on the list, and the evening after that, and the evening after that, is what actually dismantled a four-item freeze that had, in aggregate, been standing for years.

A second scene shows this same mechanism deployed more formally, worth including because it demonstrates the principle scales up deliberately rather than only working by accident. A financial advisor, working with a client who's described, across several sessions, a familiar pattern of good intentions that never quite convert into completed action, proposes something specific at the end of their third meeting: rather than leaving with another general list of things to do before the next quarterly check-in, the client commits, out loud, in the room, to a single, specific action — not "I'll look into increasing my contribution," but "I will log into the portal and change the percentage before I leave this parking lot today" — with the advisor waiting, deliberately, for a text confirming it's been done before the meeting is considered complete. The client does it, in the parking lot, in under two minutes, a task that had been sitting undone, in various half-formed versions, for the better part of a year.

A third scene closes this chapter's opening set, worth including because it shows the same mechanism working entirely without professional help, built by an ordinary reader applying nothing more than what this book has already covered. A man in his fifties, recognizing three separate chapters of this book in his own life at once, decides against tackling all three simultaneously, remembering the specific caution against exactly that impulse. Instead, he opens his calendar, right there while reading, and creates three separate entries, each on a different evening over the following ten days, each with a single line describing the smallest possible first step for one item — "find the old 401k login," "draft the beneficiary form, don't submit," "text my brother to set a specific date for the buy-sell conversation." He closes the book for the evening having taken no action on any of the underlying decisions themselves. Ten days later, following through on each small calendar entry in turn, all three items have moved from frozen to genuinely in motion — not resolved, but no longer stuck, which turns out to be the harder and more important threshold to cross.

What's actually happening

The economist Thomas Schelling, whose work on strategic decision-making and commitment eventually contributed to a Nobel Memorial Prize in Economic Sciences, developed and popularized the concept of commitment devices — mechanisms by which a person, acting now, deliberately narrows their own future options in order to guarantee a specific future behavior, precisely because they anticipate, correctly, that their future self, facing the decision in the moment, might not follow through on an intention formed today. Schelling's foundational work, dating to his 1956 paper on the strategy of conflict and developed further in subsequent research, was originally framed around negotiation and deterrence, but its core insight applies with unusual precision to every chapter in this book: a person's intentions, formed at a calm moment with full information, are a genuinely poor predictor of that same person's actual behavior at the moment action is required, specifically because the calm, informed self and the busy, avoidant, in-the-moment self are, functionally, making two different decisions under two very different conditions — and Schelling's research suggests the solution isn't to somehow make the future self more disciplined. It's to have the present self build a structure that makes the correct action nearly automatic by the time the future self encounters it.

This reframes everything this book has covered. Every override offered across the previous nine chapters — the pre-committed rollover deadline, the automatic rebalancing setting, the assigned owner for a shared decision, the fixed decision date for a maximizing search — is, in Schelling's terms, a commitment device: a structure built by a calm, motivated version of the reader, in advance, specifically because that calm, motivated version correctly anticipated that a later, less motivated version would need the structure already in place rather than needing to generate the motivation fresh, in the moment, from nothing.

There's a closely related and highly practical body of research worth introducing directly in this final chapter, from the psychologist Peter Gollwitzer, whose extensive work on what he termed implementation intentions, beginning in the mid-1990s and replicated across a large number of subsequent studies, found something specific and remarkably powerful about how intentions actually convert into completed action. Gollwitzer's research distinguished between a goal intention — a general statement of what someone wants to achieve, such as "I want to roll over my old account" — and an implementation intention, a specific, if-then plan that names both a precise triggering moment and a precise action, such as "if it's Tuesday evening after dinner, then I will call the plan provider." Across Gollwitzer's studies and the many replications that followed, people who formed specific implementation intentions completed their intended actions at substantially higher rates than people who formed only a general goal intention, even when both groups reported identical levels of motivation and identical understanding of what needed to be done. The gap between knowing what to do and doing it — the exact gap this entire book has been describing — is, per Gollwitzer's research, closed far more reliably by a specific if-then plan than by any amount of additional motivation, willpower, or understanding.

It's worth being precise about why the five-minute commitment in this chapter's opening scene worked, in Gollwitzer's terms specifically: it wasn't a vague goal intention ("I'll work on my finances"). It was a genuine, if modest, implementation intention — a specific time (that evening), a specific trigger (before bed), and a specific, narrowly bounded action (five minutes, on one item). Gollwitzer's research suggests this specificity is doing almost all of the actual work. The action succeeded not because five minutes happens to be an inherently powerful unit of time, but because naming a precise trigger and a precise, bounded action removes the exact ambiguity — when, exactly, will I do this, and what, exactly, does "doing it" require — that every previous chapter has identified as the specific gap where the status quo bias, the omission bias, the maximizing search, and every other mechanism this book has covered actually take hold and win.

There's a final piece worth naming, tying the whole book together: every single mechanism covered across the previous nine chapters — status quo bias, choice overload, omission bias, anticipated regret and mortality salience, default effects, procrastination and diffused responsibility, maximizing versus satisficing, short-term regret asymmetry, and accumulated decision fatigue — shares one structural vulnerability in common, and Schelling's and Gollwitzer's research both point at it directly: all of them operate most powerfully against large, ambiguous, emotionally loaded, effort-intensive tasks, and all of them lose most of their power against a task that's been shrunk down to something small, specific, time-bound, and pre-committed in advance. You don't need ten different strategies for ten different kinds of paralysis. You need one underlying move, applied consistently: take whatever the frozen decision actually is, and build, today, while you're calm and motivated and reading a book that's made the mechanism visible to you, the smallest possible specific commitment that gets the version of you who'll actually face the moment to have somewhere obvious and low-effort to start.

There's a further piece of Gollwitzer's research worth adding, because it addresses a specific, reasonable objection: doesn't naming a precise trigger just create one more thing to forget or dismiss, the same way the man's rebalancing reminder in Chapter 5 got dismissed a dozen times? Gollwitzer's own studies anticipated this concern directly and found something important — the effectiveness of an implementation intention doesn't come from the reminder itself, but from the mental act of forming the specific if-then link in the first place. His research, using tools that measured automatic attention and response speed, found that people who'd formed a genuine implementation intention responded faster and more automatically to the specified trigger when it actually arrived, even without any external reminder present at all, compared to people who'd only formed a general goal. The if-then structure appears to create something closer to a genuine automatic association in memory, not merely a note to be seen and potentially ignored — which is precisely why it succeeds where a phone reminder, dismissed a dozen times over, reliably fails.

A reminder asks you to notice it and then decide. An implementation intention, formed properly, skips the deciding step almost entirely, because the deciding already happened, once, in advance, at the moment the if-then sentence was built.

What it costs you

This closing chapter inverts the structure of every previous one, because the cost worth naming here isn't the cost of one more frozen decision — it's the compounding cost of never learning the one transferable skill that would have unfrozen all of them. A person who works through this book's overrides chapter by chapter, treating each one as a separate, unrelated technique specific to its own scenario, will likely make real progress on the specific items this book happened to cover, and remain just as vulnerable to the identical freeze the next time it shows up wearing a different, unfamiliar costume — a new account, a new form, a new conversation this book never specifically described. The actual cost of missing this chapter's underlying point isn't measured in any single dollar figure. It's measured in every future frozen decision this book didn't happen to anticipate, left to work with none of the structural insight the previous nine chapters actually contained.

A second cost is specific to Gollwitzer's research: goal intentions that never convert into implementation intentions don't simply fail neutrally — per the broader body of research on unmet intentions, repeatedly forming a goal and failing to convert it into a specific plan measurably erodes a person's confidence in their own follow-through over time, making the next goal intention, even a genuinely easy one, harder to trust and therefore harder to act on. Every unconverted "I really need to get to that" is, in a small but real way, teaching you that your own stated intentions aren't reliable predictors of your own future behavior — a lesson that, left unaddressed, generalizes far beyond any single account or form.

A third and final cost ties back to where this book began: every chapter in this book described people who were, by any ordinary measure, capable, informed, and sincere in their intentions. None of them lacked knowledge. What they lacked, consistently, was the specific structural move this closing chapter has finally named directly. The cost of not learning it isn't a character flaw catching up with them — it's the ordinary, universal gap between knowing and doing, left unaddressed, quietly determining the outcome of decision after decision, for years, regardless of how much any of them genuinely wanted to act. That gap doesn't close on its own, no matter how long you wait for it to, and no matter how many times you form the same good intention hoping this time will be different.

The overrides

Build one implementation intention, in the exact if-then format Gollwitzer's research validated, for the single most pressing item on your own list. Not "I'll deal with this soon." A specific sentence: "If it is [specific day and time], then I will [specific, narrowly bounded action]." Write it down. Put it somewhere you'll actually see it at the specified time — a calendar entry, not just a mental note, since a mental note is precisely the kind of vague goal intention Gollwitzer's research found least likely to convert into action.

The Move: pick the single smallest possible action available for your most-frozen decision, right now, and do it within the next five minutes, before finishing this book. Not tomorrow. Not after you've finished reading. This chapter has made the mechanism as clear as it's going to get, and the specific research behind it — Schelling's commitment devices, Gollwitzer's implementation intentions — both point at the same conclusion: the gap between understanding a mechanism and acting on it is exactly the gap this entire book has described, and the fastest way to close it, once, concretely, is to close it immediately, while the understanding is freshest and the motivation this chapter just generated hasn't yet had time to fade the way every previous motivated moment in this book's scenes eventually faded.

Build your commitment devices while calm, deliberately, for every decision you can currently identify as frozen. Schelling's core insight was that the calm, present self should build structure for the future self precisely because the future self can't be relied upon to generate motivation fresh. Do this literally: sit down, once, with every item you can identify as currently frozen, and build one specific implementation intention for each — not solving each one today, just committing each one to a specific future trigger and a specific, bounded first action.

Treat every small completed action as evidence, not just progress. Following the pattern from this chapter's opening scene: each time you complete a small, pre-committed step, notice explicitly that nothing catastrophic happened, that the fear or ambiguity that had been defending the freeze didn't materialize into anything real. This isn't sentimental encouragement — it's the specific mechanism by which a five-minute action becomes a six-week resolution: each completed step is direct evidence, delivered to the part of you that actually runs these freezes, that the next step is safe to take too.

When a new frozen decision appears in your life that this book never specifically covered, apply the underlying move rather than searching for a chapter that matches. You now have the actual mechanism, not just nine scenarios. The next time you notice yourself knowing exactly what to do and not doing it, skip straight to the one move underneath every override in this book: shrink it, name a specific trigger and a specific bounded action, write it down, and do the smallest version of it now, while you're calm enough to build the structure your later self will actually need.

Teach this mechanism to one other person, deliberately, as your own final override. Explaining the gap between knowing and doing to someone else — a partner, a friend, an adult child watching their own account sit exactly where it's sat for years — does two things at once: it cements the mechanism in your own understanding far more durably than reading alone ever could, and it hands a second person the same structural tool this book has just handed you, at zero additional cost to either of you. Every override in this book compounds. This one compounds twice.

The Rule to Remember: You were never missing the motivation — you were missing the five minutes, named specifically, scheduled precisely, small enough that nothing in you had a reason left to say not yet.

Before You Go

Before you go, think of the one item you already know is sitting frozen in your own life right now — the one this book made you think of first, on the very first page, before you'd even finished the introduction. You knew what it was before you started reading. You still know exactly what to do about it. That hasn't changed, and it was never going to change, because this book was never written to give you information you didn't already have. It was written to explain why having it hasn't been enough.

If you've read this cover to cover, notice something about the shape of what you just read: ten chapters, ten different accounts and forms and conversations, and not one of them was a story about someone who didn't know better. Every single person in these pages knew better. The woman with the spreadsheet. The man with the beneficiary form. The couple who couldn't finish a car-ride conversation across six years. The consultant comparing five good insurance plans he'd already found. None of them needed a lecture on why the correct action mattered. They needed something this book has tried to give you directly: a name for the specific mechanism standing between knowing and doing, and a small, concrete way to build around it rather than waiting to feel ready to push through it.

You've watched ten versions of the same underlying event, dressed in different financial clothes each time. The status quo defending itself simply by requiring no effort to remain in place. Too many good options collapsing into no decision at all. The fear of an active mistake outweighing the certain cost of an inactive one. A document that requires confronting something painful before it can be signed. An allocation drifting because staying put was always the default. A conversation that reopens constantly and closes never. A search for the perfect option standing in the way of any good one. A window of easy, costless progress closing quietly while nobody was watching for it to close. A backlog of small, individually simple items growing heavy through sheer accumulation. And finally, the one move that actually breaks all of it: not motivation, not willpower, not finally feeling ready, but a specific, small, pre-committed action, named precisely enough that there was nowhere left for the freeze to hide.

It's worth being honest about what this book has not promised. It hasn't promised that every decision you unfreeze will turn out, in hindsight, to have been unambiguously the right one — genuine uncertainty about the future is real, and no amount of overcoming paralysis converts an uncertain decision into a guaranteed one. What this book has argued, instead, is narrower and more useful: that a good decision made today, imperfectly, is worth more than a perfect decision endlessly deferred, and that the freeze standing between you and action was never really protecting you from a wrong choice. It was protecting you from the discomfort of choosing at all, and that discomfort, examined honestly, chapter after chapter, turns out to be considerably smaller and more survivable than the years of accumulated cost it's been quietly guarding.

It's also worth naming, honestly, what this book cannot do for you, because false promises don't serve anyone well in a book about facing reality directly. This book cannot make the specific decision for you — it cannot tell you which fund to choose, which coverage level fits your family, what your will should actually say. That work belongs to you and, where appropriate, to the professionals equipped to help you do it properly. What this book can do, and has tried to do across every one of these ten chapters, is clear the specific obstacle that's kept you from getting to that work in the first place — the freeze itself, not the decision behind it. Once the freeze lifts, the actual decisions ahead of you are, in the overwhelming majority of cases, considerably more straightforward than the years of avoidance made them feel.

If you found yourself recognizing more than one chapter — and most readers do — resist the urge to tackle all of it at once, tempting as that impulse might feel in this moment of fresh clarity. Chapter 10 named this trap directly: a four-item list attacked all at once looks like one enormous, undifferentiated task, exactly the shape this book has spent its whole length showing you gets deferred. Pick one. Name the smallest version of it. Do that smallest version this week. Let the second item wait its turn, with its own scheduled implementation intention, rather than trying to prove something to yourself by clearing your entire list in a single burst of motivation that, per every chapter in this book, is unlikely to still be running by Thursday.

Here is the whole book, compressed into the sentence it was always building toward: the freeze isn't a failure of information — it's your mind quietly voting for the status quo because inaction feels, falsely, like the one choice you can't get wrong, and the only reliable way through it is not to want it more, but to make the correct action smaller, more specific, and more automatic than the freeze has ever had to be.

So here is the one practice to carry out of these pages, the same one this book's final chapter asked of you directly: pick the item you thought of on the first page. Name the smallest possible next step. Give it a specific day, a specific time, a specific bounded action — five minutes is enough, it was always enough. Write it down somewhere you'll actually see it. And then, before this book closes for good, take that first small step, however small, and notice, afterward, that you're still exactly the same person you were before you took it — just one step closer to being someone who finally moved the money you always knew you should move.

Notes & Further Reading

The psychological and behavioral-economics concepts referenced throughout this book draw on established, verifiable research. Readers interested in going deeper are pointed toward the original sources and researchers credited in each chapter, rather than toward secondary summaries. Where a chapter names a specific paper, journal, or year, that detail is provided so the interested reader can locate the original work directly rather than relying on this book's own paraphrase of it — a deliberate choice, since a secondhand description of a study is never a substitute for reading the study itself, and this book would rather point you toward the real source than ask you to simply trust its own retelling.

On status quo bias: Economists William Samuelson and Richard Zeckhauser's 1988 research, published in the *Journal of Risk and Uncertainty*, identifying and naming the systematic preference for maintaining a current arrangement over switching to an objectively equal or better alternative, underlies the discussion in Chapter 1 of why an old retirement account so reliably stays exactly where it is.

On default effects in retirement savings: Economists Brigitte Madrian and Dennis Shea's 2001 study, published in the *Quarterly Journal of Economics*, examining how automatic enrollment dramatically increased retirement plan participation compared to opt-in enrollment, underlies the same chapter's discussion of how defaults govern outcomes independent of underlying preference.

On choice overload: Psychologists Sheena Iyengar and Mark Lepper's 2000 study, published in the *Journal of Personality and Social Psychology* and widely known as the "jam study," documenting how a smaller set of options produced dramatically higher purchase rates than a larger set, underlies the discussion in Chapter 2 of why more good investment options can produce less action rather than more.

On maximizing versus satisficing: Economist Herbert Simon's foundational 1956 work on bounded rationality, and psychologist Barry Schwartz's subsequent research with colleagues (including a 2002 paper co-authored with Andrew Ward, John Monterosso, Sonja Lyubomirsky, Katherine White, and Darrin Lehman, published in the *Journal of Personality and*

Social Psychology) distinguishing maximizing from satisficing decision styles and their differing relationships to regret and satisfaction, underlies the discussion in Chapters 2 and 7.

On omission bias: Psychologists Ilana Ritov and Jonathan Baron's research beginning in 1990, and their subsequent 1991 study with Mark Spranca and Elisa Minsk published in the *Journal of Experimental Social Psychology*, documenting the systematic preference for harm caused by inaction over equivalent or greater harm caused by action, underlies the discussion in Chapter 3 of why an outdated form can feel safer to leave alone than to correct.

On anticipated regret and "risk as feelings": Economist George Loewenstein's 2001 paper with Elke Weber, Christopher Hsee, and Ned Welch, published in *Psychological Bulletin*, documenting how anticipated emotional experience often governs decision-making more powerfully than calculated probability, underlies the discussion in Chapter 4 of why a will's guardianship clause is so much harder to write than its statistical likelihood would suggest.

On mortality salience and terror management theory: The research program developed by social psychologists Jeff Greenberg, Sheldon Solomon, and Tom Pyszczynski beginning in 1986, examining how direct reminders of mortality produce measurable avoidance behavior, underlies the same chapter's discussion of why a will is structurally unlike most other financial documents.

On regret theory and decision commitment: Psychologists Terry Connolly and Marcel Zeelenberg's research on anticipated regret and the specific discomfort of the moment of commitment, distinct from a decision's broader content, underlies the same chapter's discussion of why naming a concrete plan feels harder than discussing one in the abstract.

On default effects and organ donation: Economists Eric Johnson and Daniel Goldstein's 2003 study, published in *Science*, comparing organ donor participation rates under opt-in versus opt-out registration systems, underlies the discussion in Chapter 5 of why an allocation, once set, tends to stay exactly as it was set regardless of underlying preference.

On automatic escalation and Save More Tomorrow: Economists Richard Thaler and Shlomo Benartzi's 2004 paper, published in the *Journal of Political Economy*, describing a program that pre-committed employees to automatic future contribution increases, underlies the same chapter's discussion of restructuring which option gets to be the default.

On procrastination and temporal motivation theory: Organizational psychologist Piers Steel's 2007 meta-analysis, published in *Psychological Bulletin*, synthesizing decades of procrastination research into a framework describing how uncertainty, discomfort, and the absence of a hard deadline predict chronic task deferral, underlies the discussion in Chapter 6.

On the Zeigarnik effect: Psychologist Bluma Zeigarnik's original 1927 research documenting that incomplete or interrupted tasks are remembered and mentally revisited more than completed ones underlies the discussion in Chapters 6 and 9 of why an unresolved conversation or an accumulating backlog keeps resurfacing without ever closing.

On diffusion of responsibility: Social psychologists Bibb Latané and John Darley's foundational studies from the late 1960s on why shared responsibility reduces individual likelihood of action underlies the discussion in Chapter 6 of why shared financial conversations stall between well-intentioned people.

On Hick's Law: The independent research of William Hick and Ray Hyman in the early 1950s establishing that decision time increases measurably with the number of available options underlies the discussion in Chapters 7 and 9 of why closely matched options can produce more paralysis than clearly differentiated ones.

On the temporal pattern of regret: Psychologists Thomas Gilovich and Victoria Medvec's 1994 study, published in the *Journal of Personality and Social Psychology*, documenting the reversal between short-term action regret and long-term inaction regret, underlies the discussion in Chapter 8 of why a costless, beneficial change is so easy to let lapse.

On mental accounting: Economist Richard Thaler's foundational research on how people assign money to non-fungible mental categories, and how those categories shape spending behavior, underlies the same chapter's discussion of why newly freed-up or newly arriving money is especially vulnerable to gradual reabsorption into ordinary spending.

On hedonic adaptation: Psychologist Philip Brickman's foundational research, with colleagues, on how quickly people adjust to a new financial or circumstantial baseline underlies the same chapter's discussion of why a raise stops feeling like extra money within weeks of arriving.

On commitment devices: Economist Thomas Schelling's foundational 1956 work on strategic commitment, part of the research recognized in his share of the 2005 Nobel Memorial Prize in Economic Sciences, underlies the discussion in Chapter 10 of why a calm, motivated present self should build structure in advance for a future self that can't be relied upon to generate the same motivation fresh.

On implementation intentions: Psychologist Peter Gollwitzer's research beginning in the mid-1990s, and the substantial body of replication that followed, distinguishing general goal intentions from specific if-then implementation intentions and documenting the latter's significantly higher completion rates, underlies the same chapter's central practical framework.

This book does not cite any statistic, study, or finding not directly attributable to a named researcher and a real, published body of work. Readers are encouraged to consult the primary sources above for the full depth of the underlying research.

This book addresses ordinary, non-clinical decision-avoidance and chronic deferral around money — the account left unrolled, the form left unsigned, the conversation left unfinished — and it is not a substitute for professional mental health support. If your difficulty acting on financial decisions is connected to a broader pattern of anxiety, depression, or a diagnosed condition that affects decision-making generally, please seek support from a licensed therapist or counselor. This book is also not financial, legal, insurance, or tax advice. It does not recommend any specific investment, account, allocation, insurance product, or legal structure, and nothing in it should be treated as a substitute for guidance from a qualified financial advisor, estate attorney, or insurance professional familiar with your specific circumstances. Its subject is behavioral: the psychology of why a fully informed decision so often goes unmade, not the question of what any particular reader's correct decision should actually be.

About

The Paralysis Instinct is part of a library exploring the wired-in patterns that shape how people relate to money — not as a series of character flaws to overcome through willpower, but as a set of honest, researched mechanisms built into every human nervous system, worth understanding on their own terms. Each book in the library isolates one distinct pattern, traces it to its real psychological roots, and offers concrete, decision-level ways to work with it rather than against it.

Every book in this library is built the same way: one pattern, traced honestly to real research, translated into overrides you can actually use under pressure rather than only in hindsight. None of them promise to remove the pattern they describe. All of them are trying to do the one thing that actually holds up under real conditions — widen the gap between the moment the pattern fires and the moment you act on it, until there's room in that gap for the calmer, more complete version of you to have a say.

None of these books ask you to become a different kind of person. They ask you to notice, honestly and without judgment, which specific pattern tends to run the show when the decision arrives — and then to build one small, concrete piece of structure around that specific pattern, in advance, while you're calm enough to build it well. That's the entire method, repeated across every pattern this library covers. It isn't dramatic. It doesn't promise transformation. It just quietly works, one widened gap at a time, which turns out to be exactly the kind of unglamorous, durable progress that actually holds up on the days that matter most.

If this book helped you see your own frozen decision clearly, even once, the next useful step is simple: pick the smallest version of it, give it a specific time, and do it before you close this book for good. That's the whole practice. It doesn't get more complicated than that, and it doesn't need to.

You were never missing the answer. You were missing the five minutes. Go take them.

Also in the Series

Every book in The Money Instinct library stands on its own — read them in any order. If this one was useful, the library continues:

The Money Instinct

The Secrecy Instinct

The Underearning Instinct

The Shame Instinct

The Panic Instinct

The Merge Instinct

The Ceiling Instinct

The Windfall Instinct

The Control Instinct

The Legacy Instinct

The Comparison Instinct

The Enabling Instinct

The Austerity Instinct

The Retirement Instinct

The Divorce Instinct

The Enough Instinct

The Overconfidence Instinct

The Vigilance Instinct

The Generosity Instinct